D0406749

A PATCH OF EDEN

A PATCH

America's Inner-City Gardeners

OF EDEN

H. PATRICIA HYNES

CHELSEA GREEN PUBLISHING COMPANY

WHITE RIVER JUNCTION, VERMONT

Copyright © 1996 Institute on Women and Technology.
Unless otherwise noted, photographs are copyright © 1996 H. Patricia Hynes.
All rights reserved.
Thanks to the National Gardening Association for use of photos
on pages vi, 10, 23, 43, 137, and 158.

No part of this book may be transmitted in any form by any means without permission
in writing from the publisher.

Designed by Ann Aspell
Calligraphy by Rene Schall

Printed in the United States of America
00 99 98 97 96   1 2 3 4 5

Library of Congress Cataloging-in-Publication Data
Hynes, H. Patricia
A patch of Eden : America's inner city gardeners / H. Patricia Hynes.
      p.   cm.
Includes bibliographical references and index.
ISBN 0–930031–80–6
1. Community gardens—United States.   I. Title.
                       SB457.3.H95   1996
307.76'2—dc20   96–11886

CHELSEA GREEN PUBLISHING COMPANY
P.O. Box 428
White River Junction, Vermont 05001

CONTENTS

INTRODUCTION

Our cities—old and new—do not only need to be fixed, they also need to be reimagined . . . places where we live can be places of hope.

—Martin J. Rosen

I GREW UP WITH STORIES OF MY RESOURCEFUL POLISH GRANDMOTHER, WHO kept geese and pigs in her small, compact backyard in working-class Perth Amboy, New Jersey. Each spring she plucked the goosedown with which she made comforters for her seven children. My Ukrainian grandfather smoked meat in a backyard shed, and collected wild mushrooms every autumn in nearby North Jersey woodlands. Together they canned homegrown fruits and vegetables, and stored apples and a variety of root crops from their garden in a section of the cellar left unfinished and unheated to serve as a root cellar. Like thousands who emigrated from European towns and villages to crowded American cities, these two were urban and of modest income; but they lived with an independence that seems out of reach today.

The decline and death of many American cities is writ large in the exodus from cities to suburbs of the grandchildren of this immigrant generation in the 1950s; in the razing of once-vibrant urban neighborhoods for highway projects; and in the failure of urban renewal in the 1960s and 1970s to revitalize inner-city downtowns. The periodic riots in Washington, D.C., Detroit, Los Angeles, New Haven, and dozens of other cities signify the "no-exit" life of people stuck in ghettos.

Nevertheless, side-by-side with decay, neglect, and disintegration, we can also see a contrasting, if tentative, neighborhood revitalization occurring, variously known as Roses in Roxbury (Boston), the Greening of Harlem, Cabrini Greens (Chicago), the Heritage Eight and Busy Bee Gardens (North Philadelphia), the Garden of Happiness (South Bronx), and the Garden Project (Hunter's Point, San Francisco). The modest but vibrant community garden movement in low-income neighborhoods and ghettos throughout the United States is the subject of this book. Urban community gardeners are bringing life and livability, seed by seed, back to their neighborhoods.

In May 1992, I was part of an audience watching a slide show presented by the Boston Urban Gardeners. We saw city lots that were once wastelands, and that are now oases of rose arbors, fruit trees, and vegetable and herb gardens. What moved many to tears was not only the profound transformation of blight to beauty (although the alchemy takes one's breath away), but the stories of those who were the instigators and unrelenting pulse of each garden—stories I have since chronicled as they unfold in inner cities across the United States. Their stories are the heart of this book.

As I watched the slide show, the country was still reeling from the explosion of rage in South Central Los Angeles after the Rodney King verdict. The epicenter was Los Angeles, but aftershocks reverberated in every city and town in the United States. With few exceptions, the urban policy "experts" with whom I was teaching in the Department of Urban Studies and Planning at MIT were wordless, speechless, clueless—devoid of idea, analysis, or constructive policy— about the complex anger the country witnessed. Decades of expert theory about model cities, the war on poverty, downtown revitalization, enterprise zones, crime and gang control, and the hardening divide between black and white, seemed to vaporize in the heat of the burning city.

The stories of community gardens in Roxbury, Dorchester, and the South End of Boston implied an innovative kind of urban renewal, one undertaken with the cheapest of resources: seeds, soil, and the sweat equity of inner-city people. The slides chronicled a revolution accomplished with trowels, spades, and rototillers, and one instigated in large part by women. This low-cost, low-tech urban renewal relies on intangibles like beauty and a sense of place, as well as tangibles like food and neighborhood security. Phrases such as *open space, greenspace,* and *urban amenity*—the professional argot of urban planners—fail to convey the potency of these garden movements. *Urban renaissance* comes closer to capturing the complex effect of these community gardens, which nourish the body and also the soul.

The photographic images I saw that spring of 1992 drew me irresistibly away from a position of academic expertise in Cambridge to face-to-face visits with the local social geniuses who are at work greening Harlem, North Philadelphia, a public housing project in Chicago, and the county jail of San Francisco. In these gardens I saw cities reimagined and rehabilitated, lot by lot in some cases, block by block in others, and even acre by acre. In these gardens, a measure of human hope—the first and only for some gardeners—is being restored. My

Amtrak trips from Boston to Harlem in fall 1992 came to symbolize for me the reversal at work in this book.

En route from South Station to Penn Station, I would shut off the mental playback of my colleagues' discourses on persistent poverty and "the underclass," and instead prepare questions about the future of inner cities for people who are creating it.

Between Wilderness and Lawn

A garden might be seen as a minor, merely local, and cosmetic experience of nature that could be more authentically sought in wild and remote places. Yet gardens, comments Michael Pollan, with their "middle ground between the wilderness and the lawn," may "suggest the lineaments of a new environmental ethic . . . and help us out in all those situations where the wilderness ethic is silent or unhelpful," or where the experience of wilderness is unaffordable and inaccessible.

The women and men you will meet within this book offer a new kind of environmental ethic and urban renewal, one based on an urban ecology and a low-income but resilient economy. Their ecology is predicated not on wilderness without people but on a mutuality between humans and nature; their economy is predicated on traditional finance, sweat equity, barter, and non-monetary sources of wealth such as networks, good will, generosity, altruism, plant lore, and horticultural expertise.

And prescient they are. For while the world has become increasingly urban—by the year 2000 more than 50 percent of the world's population will live in cities—the majority of environmental activism and research has been decidedly non-urban in focus. In the National Academy of Sciences' 1988 volume *Biodiversity* only six pages out of 496 were devoted to urban biodiversity. A major 1987 tricentennial symposium at Clark University entitled *The Earth as Transformed by Human Action: Global and Regional Changes in the Biosphere over the Past 300 Years* documented broad changes in the biosphere, but noted urbanized regions only incidentally. The International Institute for Environment and Development documents that international aid and development agencies allocate between 15 and 20 percent of their funds to urban areas. Likewise, the landmark United Nations Conference on Environment and Development, held in Rio de Janiero in 1992, devoted only one out of forty chapters in its official consensus document, *Agenda 21*, to cities. And in his highly acclaimed book *Earth in the Balance* Vice President Al Gore failed to address the topic of cities as human habitats

Community gardens in American cities are not altogether new. However, their purposes today—neither charity, nor philanthropy, nor war relief—are. Their goals include teaching children horticulture and diverting them from the streets; cleaning up overgrown neighborhood eyesores and pushing out drug dealing that, like weeds, overtakes neglected vacant lots; growing and preserving food from seed to shelf; restoring nature to the industrial city using heirloom plants and bird and butterfly gardens; and, in one instance, bringing the farming tradition of rural Mississippi to urban Philadelphia. These are but a handful of the reasons that urban gardeners have given when asked why they garden. At its core, the community garden movement in the late twentieth century is about rebuilding neighborhood community and restoring ecology to the inner city. Some gardens are linked to housing projects, others to local markets; still others employ people who are incarcerated or recently released from jail. Even where the legacy of philanthropy lingers, such as in the instance of Philadelphia foundations and the Pennsylvania Horticulture Society, which invest in citywide community garden projects, it has lost the odor of reform charity—of the "haves" uplifting the "have nots"—that characterized earlier garden movements in cities.

Charity Gardens and Victory Gardens

One hundred years ago, Detroit Mayor Hazen S. Pingree asked owners of vacant land at the edge of that city to lend their property for the urban unemployed to farm. The economic depression of 1893–1897 had hit the railway car manufacturing sector of Detroit badly. The city plowed 455 acres of plots and provided seed potatoes for 945 families, each of whom was given an allotment garden between one-quarter and one-half acre in size. In the fall of 1894, gardeners harvested beans, turnips, other vegetables, and fourteen thousand bushels of potatoes. Twelve thousand dollars worth of crops were raised from a three thousand dollar investment: The program saved the city's Poor Commission nine thousand dollars in food welfare purchases.

Pingree's potato patches were imitated throughout the country, and by 1895 twenty other cities, including Chicago, Buffalo, Denver, Seattle, Boston, and Providence, had similar poverty relief programs. But those garden programs for the urban poor were short-lived and on a smaller scale than Detroit's. Food production by unemployed people could not compete with real estate development, which historically has been the preferred use of vacant land in American cities. Thus, any upswing in building activity took precedence over the loan of vacant lots to the poor for charity gardens. City beautification further displaced urban self-help. Municipalities preferred to dedicate public land designated for open space to elegant pastoral parks, rather than lease it for populist potato patches. Turn-of-the-century garden allotments for the poor were short-lived, surviving no more than five or ten years.

World War I stimulated a revival of urban gardens during 1917, 1918, and 1919. This time, instead of charity relief, patriotic slogans buttressed the nation-wide effort. A national campaign with posters and press releases encouraged people at home to serve the war effort with "liberty gardens," and then with postwar "victory gardens," while food from commercial agriculture was sent to feed soldiers and European allies. An estimated five million gardeners, rallying to such slogans as "plant for freedom" and "hoe for liberty," grew $520,000,000 worth of food in 1918. In England, 1.5 million gardeners kept that country from starving during the German submarine blockade.

Once again, when the postwar economy revived real estate development, urban gardens were abolished to make way for construction projects. Throughout the 1920s and 1930s, modest efforts were made to incorporate community and allotment gardens into urban subsistence programs and new city and town design. During the Depression, the Work Projects Administration (WPA) sponsored "relief gardens" on vacant city lots for unemployed and indigent people. In New York City the welfare department and the WPA sponsored a project of nearly five thousand gardens on the equivalent of seven hundred acres. However, the federal government abandoned the relief garden program in 1937 when the United States Department of Agriculture (USDA) initiated a food stamp program for farm-surplus products. Serious community gardening was not revived until World War II.

The iconic victory garden—skillfully promoted at the end of World War I by the National War Garden Commission to sustain community gardens during lean postwar years—was well established in national memory when the United States entered World War II. In the early 1940s citizens plowed and cultivated nearly all available land, including town commons and city parks, green strips around industrial plants, church and school grounds, backyards, and vacant lots, to support the war effort. Seed companies packaged and marketed seed packs for the victory garden with advertising slogans such as "marching to victory via the victory garden." As in World War I, gardeners at home fed their households—for national security, economy, and health—while commercial farmers fed soldiers and the Allies, whose agriculture was disrupted by war. At their most productive in 1944, victory gardens produced 44 percent of the fresh vegetables eaten in the United States.

The legendary Fenway gardens in Boston were first established as victory gardens in the spring of 1942 on seven-and-a-half acres of land owned by the Boston Parks Department. They live on today as some four hundred vegetable and flower gardens, each measuring an average of fifteen-by-twenty-five feet, whose gardeners reflect the diversity of the neighborhood's gay and senior citizen communities. Few community gardens have enjoyed the longevity of the Fenway Garden Society, except perhaps the postwar gardens of Berlin.

Four percent of Berlin is still gardened on land that people reclaimed after World War II from the rubble left by bombing raids. Today, more than eighty thousand gardeners lease plots on eight thousand acres for their *kleingartens* (little gardens). But development-minded bureaucrats are now threatening to close many of the Berlin gardens in prime areas near the Kurfürstendamm in order to develop the land for real estate. They have calculated that they could develop $650 million worth of real estate on half of the garden land. Environmentalists there argue that the gardens of Berlin make the city more livable and valuable. Gardeners like Hannelore Schmidt, who tends fruit trees and herb and vegetable gardens on land leased from the city, two blocks from the Kurfürstendamm, cannot imagine living in Berlin without the garden. "This garden," she said, "is the center of my life . . . I have a close feeling for God, and I think this is it."

The Cornell Oasis in Chicago, comprising slightly less than four acres in a dense, congested residential area in east Hyde Park, has been gardened for fifty years. The original victory gardens at the Cornell Oasis have become twenty highly individual vegetable, flower, and naturalized gardens with mature trees, where seventeen species of butterflies and dozens of species of birds have been sighted. The Oasis, too, is now threatened with a proposal to develop sixty townhouses on its land. The struggle of gardeners there to save this tiny wildlife habitat and human retreat exemplifies the conflicting agendas that have plagued the history of community gardens: of real estate developers versus those who favor "non-market" or so-called "less valuable" uses of land.

During the postwar transition of the late 1940s and early 1950s, most community gardens were abandoned; and newspapers and garden magazines began to promote manicured lawns for the new suburban yard. During the next half-century, mowed lawns, golf courses, and landscaped plantings around corporate centers would come to dominate the American landscape, all maintained with the aid of the pesticides first produced for mosquito and lice control in World War II, and subsequently promoted as "magic bullets" for civilian agriculture and horticulture. At the margins, however, intermittent and independent garden activities did spring up throughout the 1950s, 1960s, and 1970s, some of which generated the momentum culminating in the community garden movement of our inner cities today.

A Movement of Many

In the 1950s and 1960s public housing authorities in Chicago, New York, and Philadelphia promoted garden clubs among tenants for purposes of beautification. In 1974, Ernesta Drinker Ballard, a prominent horticulturalist, founded Philadelphia Green with the express philosophy of breaking with the model of charity that had characterized horticulture society and garden club projects of the previous decades. Instead, the programs she initiated emphasized self-help and reciprocity between the greening organization and the gardener. By 1994, Philadelphia Green had assisted low- and middle-income urban neighborhoods to establish more than two thousand community gardens.

At the same time that Ballard was starting up Philadelphia's greening program, black activist politican Mel King was sponsoring the Massachusetts Gardening and Farm Act of 1974, to enable urban gardeners and farmers to grow food rent-free on vacant public land. By 1995, three thousand households had produced an estimated $1.5 million worth of food in Boston's 120 community garden projects. In the mid-1970s a handful of landscape professionals in New York City formed the Green Guerrillas to assist people who wanted to start gardens on vacant lots. By 1985 they had established over one thousand gardens.

In 1976, the United States Department of Agriculture initiated an urban gardening program in six cities to assist low-income people to grow and preserve vegetables. By 1993 the program had grown to include twenty-three cities, where two hundred thousand urban gardeners grew an average of six dollars worth of vegetables for every dollar invested by the USDA. Today a fifteen-by-fifteen-foot plot, gardened intensively, can provide its gardeners with up to five hundred dollars worth of food over a growing season.

In 1978 community gardeners and organizers from all parts of the country met in Chicago and formed the American Community Gardening Association (ACGA), to promote community gardening in urban, suburban, and rural America as a tool for political organizing and community development. Between 1990 and 1992, 523 new community gardens were started in twenty-four cities, according to ACGA's National Community Gardening Survey. The ACGA estimates that there are 250 to 500 citywide community gardening programs in the United States, and the organization receives hundreds of requests annually for technical assistance in starting up new community garden projects.

Thousands of tributaries, emanating from the civil rights, women's liberation, environmental, and social justice movements, feed this broad-based national community garden movement. Despite its disparate and seemingly uncoordinated beginnings in the 1970s, it is a movement whose members share common feelings, ideals, and goals about the power of gardens. Charles Lewis, a garden advocate, describes community gardens as "the glue that holds a block together until long-term economic and social development can take place." Dozens of projects teach unemployed and unskilled teenagers, pregnant teenagers, homeless people, and inmates how to create a garden. "For many," says Cathrine Sneed, who started an eight-acre organic farm at the San Francisco County Jail in San Bruno, "this is the first dirt they can wash off."

All the urban gardeners I have met in the course of writing this book have said, in one way or another, that what they love about gardening is that gardens give back. This mutuality between humans and nature—experienced in the mundane tasks of sowing, weeding, transplanting, and watering—reveals the capacity of urban gardens for teaching ecological literacy, a literacy that changes how people live, not merely how they think and talk.

Soil and City Life

Horticulture has always been practiced in cities: In our ancestors' transition from nomadic to settled existence, gardens eventually gave birth to cities. The earliest gardens were sited on riverine plains and deltas that were renewed by the annual silt-bearing floods of the Nile, the Tigris and Euphrates, the Indus, the Yangtze, and the Hwang-Ho. From the surplus wealth of alluvial soil, farmers built the first cities. For thousands of years, built and cultivated environments coexisted: Homes, markets, public buildings, and sacred spaces were interspersed with kitchen gardens, farms, and common grazing land for animals. Not until the Industrial Revolution were dooryard and market gardens, orchards, and town commons usurped by brick, mortar, and asphalt. Banishing nature was "not the inevitable way to build cities," comments urban historian Sam Bass Warner, "but instead a bad mutation brought on by nineteenth- and twentieth-century land greed."

Horticulture, after being virtually eliminated from nineteenth-century factory neighborhoods, was then deliberately restored in selected urban open spaces (sited outside factory neighborhoods) as an antidote to the monotony, noise, congestion, and poor ventilation of industrial workplaces and tenements built for immigrants and the working class. In the mid- and late nineteenth century, large landscaped parks such as New York City's Central Park became the American city's counterpoint to the desolate, gritty factory neighborhoods that had replaced market gardens and commons.

City parks tranquilize and yet enliven, as landscape architect and Central Park designer Frederick Law Olmsted observed about the capacity of trees, meadows, ponds, and the wildlife they attract to assuage the stresses of surrounding urban life. Yet do these pastoral landscapes — ornament and elixir in congested urban America — contain adequate power to rescue their cities, as many park planners have assumed? When a neighborhood declines around one side of a park, that section of the park usually declines as well. If drug dealers move in and operate out of newly-abandoned houses, even fewer people venture past that area into the park. Having lost its constituency, the park falls lower on the priority list of the city parks department. Neglected and unmaintained, the park becomes overgrown, dark, dangerous, frightening, and abandoned by those for whom it was built. Such was the fate of Marcus Garvey and Jackie Robinson Parks in Harlem, as Chapter 1 will illustrate, until neighborhood activists and members of the Greening of Harlem reversed their destiny.

Jane Jacobs wryly observed in her 1960s commentary on the downward spiral of many city parks, that parks need people no less than people need parks. Late twentieth-century cities, however, may need local community gardens even more than they needed the grand central parks of the late nineteenth century. For the give-and-take of working in gardens attaches their gardeners to a particular place through physical and social engagement. Community gardens create relationships between city dwellers and the soil, and instill an ethic of urban environmentalism that neither parks nor wilderness—which release and free us from the industrial city—can do.

Gardens offer a more intimate and local open space than the large landscape parks can offer. Historically, only the leisured class has had time to travel frequently to central city parks; working people could only visit on Sundays and holidays. Large city parks more often became a luxurious refuge for the well-off, some of whom lived on or nearby the parks and formed parks councils and associations dedicated to aesthetic qualities, recreation, and cultural offerings. By contrast, community gardens, be they tiny "vest-pocket" sitting gardens, sidewalk tree pit gardens, or vegetable and flower gardens, bring the soothing yet enlivening power of nature to the neighborhoods where people live.

A set of questions forms the core of this book. How does the tangible—soil, plants, and trees—make possible and sustain the intangible sense of belonging to a place and a people? Can small, intensively cultivated urban gardens help people through lean economic times? In these days of tight municipal budgets, how have community gardeners financed the purchase of seeds, tools, loam, and fencing? How does the community deal with the presence of lead and other contaminants in its soil? How do gardens and the process of making them enable people to reclaim not only a drug- and rat-infested vacant lot, but a neighborhood? As one of my students asked about the synergism of gardens in low-income neighborhoods, how many small moves does it take to create a movement? Why is the Horticulture Project at the San Francisco County Jail more successful than other skills-based projects in enabling inmates to change their lives and get out of the criminal justice turnstile? Why are the prime movers of the community garden movement mainly women, and what might this mean for the future of the movement? I will use the stories of gardens and gardeners in Harlem, Chicago, San Francisco, and Philadelphia to explore these issues.

Resource economists are fidgeting to put a value on the kind of beauty and conviviality that begins with a simple corner-lot sitting garden and becomes an entire block of window boxes, streetside trees, and home improvements. They point to measures such as the enhanced property value of houses located near parks and gardens, and the fresh incentive for businesses to locate or remain in neighborhoods with gardens. Throughout this book, I have endeavored to document the myriad tangible ways that community gardens benefit inner-city neighborhoods. In addition, I have also searched for the elusive, transcendant, and nonfinancial value of those "flowers that feed the soul." The words of Jennifer Morales, who worked in a neighborhood garden on 104th Street in Spanish Harlem, are a taste of things to come:

> This garden is a paradise. Looking around the neighborhood, you wouldn't think a garden could survive there. There are old, boarded-up tenements, rundown buildings, and housing projects. There are people hanging out on the corners and cars honking all the time. But the garden is like an oasis in the desert.

In *Soil and Civilization* Edward Hyams argues that "we remain, our culture remains, our civilization remains, very much the creature of the soil we live on." Soil is more than money, he added, it is life. Is it any wonder then that as cities have sealed over their provenance with concrete and macadam, and as the word *soil* has come to mean *dirt* in the public mind, that the human and economic life of cities has ultimately ebbed from them? Is it too unorthodox to suggest that community gardeners, as they turn dirt back into soil, may again beget city life *through plant life* in late twentieth-century America, as farmers did in neolithic Asia, Africa, the Middle East, Central and South America? "Part of humanness is living in nature," says Bernadette Cozart, the founding director of the Greening of Harlem. "Gardens connect us to nature and nature connects us to the universe."

A PATCH OF EDEN

HARLEM:
Flowers Feed the Soul

PREVIOUS PAGE:
*Planting
annuals in the
garden at
PS 133.*
(Photo by Janice
Raymond)

Food feeds the body, but flowers feed the soul.
—Bernadette Cozart, Greening of Harlem Coalition

ON MOTHER'S DAY MORE FLOWERS ARE STOLEN FROM PUBLIC GARDENS than on any other day of the year. But not so in Harlem, according to Bernadette Cozart and Fred Little. Both are employed by the New York City Department of Parks and Recreation, she as a gardener and he as a landscape architect. Told by their department that gardens in Harlem would never last, the two photographed every public garden in Harlem between 2:00 and 4:00 p.m. on Mother's Day 1991 and verified that, unlike other Manhattan parks and gardens, not a petal was missing in Harlem. "Roses, small azaleas, and dahlias are plants on wheels," quipped Cozart as she explained the predilections of plant thieves. Yet the sole rose garden planted in Harlem by the Parks Department—150 Betty Prior rose bushes in Charles Young Park—is the only public rose garden in the borough that has not been vandalized. "The community that supposedly *didn't care* and *wouldn't allow the gardens to be*, has proven the Parks officials wrong," said Cozart.

The Beginnings

Prior to her assignment to Harlem, Bernadette Cozart was sent by the city to refurbish Carl Schurz Park, sixteen overgrown acres surrounding Gracie Mansion, the mayor's residence on the Upper East Side. One morning in September 1989, as she was selecting pruning tools from her garden cart, she noticed a group of black and Latino kids watching her, curious to see a woman handling loppers and saws. She asked if they wanted to help. They did; but she recalls that they were clumsy and unsure how to use her tools. "Their grandmothers grew gardens in Virginia, South Carolina, Alabama, and Puerto Rico; they kept fruit trees and put up food. But these kids didn't know how to use a shovel, loppers, or pruning saw!" When she saw one of them intimidated by garden tools, she asked, "Where's your grandmother from? Tell me about her garden. Did she grow berries and make you pies? What did she put up for the winter?" Stories of their grandmothers' gardens and orchards spilled out, and she used these stories as touchstones for teaching the kids landscaping and gardening.

Cozart used a simple ecological maxim to explain to her new apprentices why she used organic methods of horticulture. "We are all made up of the same molecules—the soil, insects, plants, you, and I. We can't harm one without harming the other." Next came her lesson on caring for plants. "This is not your football, it is not your basketball . . . you can't throw it in the closet. It's a living, breathing thing." Then followed a lesson on responsibility. "What's going to happen if you're not here to feed and water your plants?"

Once she had won their interest, Cozart hired them, seven boys and two girls, as gardeners to work under her supervision. She gave them jobs under one condition—that they go back to school.

Thus, nine fourteen-year-olds became the after-school crew of the Carl Schurz Park gardener, one of only three women gardeners in the New York City Parks Department, and the only African-American. Cozart gave her new employees a class on using tools and tool safety. She showed them how to trim trees and shrubs, how to take down invasive saplings and stump them with a grub axe and pick. Each was given her or his own plot to design, plant, weed, and prune—an idea modeled on Cozart's seminal childhood experience of tending her own school garden. Within a few months, the park contained a series of unique shade and sun gardens. Some featured bedding plants such as begonias, marigolds, and impatiens; others, a ground cover of vinca or ajuga, finished with a perimeter of hostas. Local residents and members of the Carl Schurz Park Association, who watched the gardens' progress and came to know the gardeners, hired them to trim, prune, rake, and plant in their yards, and to construct and install windowboxes. With the money they made, Cozart saw to it that her student gardeners opened savings accounts.

Bernadette watched kids beam when members of the park association complimented them on their horticulture—for some of the kids, the only positive feedback they ever got; for all of the kids, the best part of their day. "The gardens were esteem-boosters and stress-busters; they healed kids. A garden is a mini-world; making one and tending one enabled the kids to believe that they could accomplish other things elsewhere." If this worked on the Upper East Side, Cozart mused, then couldn't it—and shouldn't it—work in the kids' own neighborhoods in Central and East Harlem?

Turning a Job into a Mission

In late 1989 Bernadette Cozart was assigned by the Parks Department to Harlem to refurbish long-neglected parks and public gardens, but she was given minimal equipment, garden supplies, and staff for the job. When she insisted that she needed more resources to do her job, she met resistance and often hostility from her managers. Cozart countered her employer's neglect by looking elsewhere for financial assistance and donations of supplies. She approached local businesses, chambers of commerce, corporations, foundations, and seed and bulb companies. In the process of widening her base of support, she expanded her job as city gardener into a high-minded mission: the Greening of Harlem.

Cozart built alliances with individuals and groups in Harlem neighborhoods who wanted to create community gardens and restore local parks and playgrounds, and then formalized the network, naming it the Greening of Harlem Coalition. The Coalition members came from key community institutions, such as Harlem Hospital, Mt. Zion and St. Mary's Churches, and the Upper Room AIDS Ministry, and from local block associations and tenant groups, including the Edgecomb Avenue Block Association and Security Block 5. She welcomed into the Coalition city agencies, who assisted with services like trash pickup from vacant lots, and the Natural Resources Defense Council, which offered legal assistance in getting nonprofit status for the Greening of Harlem.

Ms. Weisberger and her fourth-grade students in Building Blocks Garden.

Today, Manhattan north of 110th Street would be grayer, barren, and dominated by cracked concrete, broken asphalt, the rubble of demolished buildings, abandoned lots choked with weeds, and the irrepressible ailanthus tree—were it not for the Greening of Harlem Coalition. To a modest, mercurial budget, add the donations from seed and bulb companies and the sweat equity of hundreds of teenagers, school children, senior citizens, and work-release prisoners. This admixture, plus the network of community leaders that Cozart brought together, and her own capacity to continue organizing and gardening (with "no office, no van, no staff, and *beyond burnout*") is the formula for the success of the Greening of Harlem.

Cozart is fond of pointing out that the Greening of Harlem is not just a seasonal, city-sponsored, city-planted, taxpayer-funded beautification program intended for passive viewing. Nor, she adds, is it the brainchild of a do-gooder anti-poverty program trying to save Harlem from itself. The Greening of Harlem rises from and thrives on neighborhood involvement. The seventeen grassroots gardens—designed, built, and tended by neighborhood people and community institutions with Cozart's guidance since 1989—are a small but potent symbol of local love and labor. This community reclamation of abandoned lots, parks, and playgrounds; the modest reversal of neighborhood disintegration; and pride in the greening of Harlem, is largely financed by the labor of Harlem people and by an informal economy based on begging, borrowing, and bartering. The story of the Greening of Harlem is fundamentally the story of an unconventional coalition of women that includes a surgeon, a homemaker turned community activist, the founder of a park conservancy, and a city parks department gardener.

Gardening, Talking, and Raising Money

"Three things are always going on in the Greening of Harlem," says Cozart: "gardening, talking to bureaucracy, and raising money." From her employer, the Department of Parks and Recreation, she gets earth-moving equipment and topsoil; from the Department of Transportation, she gets a section of concrete sidewalk jackhammered and hauled away; from the Board of Education, she gets a chain-link fence on school property taken down. "Most remarkable of all," she added, "they all came the same morning in summer 1991, and on time;" thus, the groundbreaking for the Building Blocks Playground and Garden project at Public School 197 began flawlessly.

*In the
Building
Blocks
Playground
and Garden.*

Talking to the Japanese Chamber of Commerce in New York City brought a substantial contribution to the Coalition for planting twenty-six Kwanzan flowering cherry and Callery pear trees, ninety-five shrubs, and three thousand bulbs in the perimeter garden of Harlem Hospital. The ribbon-cutting ceremony for the greening of Harlem Hospital, held on June 5, 1990, was attended by everyone important to the hospital, including staff, members of the board, and local politicians. As part of the ceremony, school children planted marigolds, begonias, and impatiens, demonstrating planting techniques to hospital administrators and guest politicians. Manhattan Borough President Ruth Messinger remarked to the audience of six hundred that this place of healing, Harlem Hospital, was also now a place of beauty.

While a hospital may seem an unlikely place to launch a community greening program, Harlem Hospital—a magnet for the community—was a natural starting point. The Uptown Chamber of Commerce meets here; so does the Pastors Association. The hospital is home to the Harlem Horizon Art Studio, where hundreds of children study art and go on to exhibit and sell their work in New York City galleries. The Harlem Dance Clinic is another hospital project, begun for young patients and now open to community children as well, whose

Children with
Fred Little, at
PS 197 garden.
Children's
mural is in the
background.

members have performed at Lincoln Center, various universities, the United Nations, and in cultural exchange programs in the Caribbean, Europe, and Russia.

Although terminally underfunded, the hospital is nonetheless a hub for the community. Resources radiate from it to dozens of community gardens, parks, and playgrounds undergoing restoration. Harlem Hospital appears side by side with the Apollo Theater and a local radio station as favorite Harlem neighborhood institutions depicted on large, vibrant murals painted by children under the direction of local artist Bryan Collier, and hung in their playgrounds and school gardens.

Pleased with the landscaping at Harlem Hospital and the public recognition they received at the ribbon-cutting ceremony, the Japanese Chamber of Commerce offered seed money to help finance another garden project. In spring 1993, the Afro-Asian Friendship Garden opened in the inner courtyard of Mary McLeod Bethune School, PS 92. Fred Little described the Afro-Asian garden as a collaboration of ideas and wishes. Rather than planting star magnolia trees, the Coalition pruned and left standing a grove of ironwood trees that shades a sitting area in the school courtyard. Classic landscape design called for smaller and more compact trees like star magnolias, whose physical form suited the courtyard space; but teachers and children were attached to the ironwoods. The sitting area was edged with chunks of pink and gray granite, recently excavated from hundreds of feet beneath van Cortland Parkway in a water tunnel construction project. (Imagine a teacher using the stone border to introduce a lesson on the bedrock that underlies Manhattan like a backbone and supports the skyscrapers clustered in midtown and the financial district). Cozart mounded soil within the granite perimeter under the ironwood trees and planted it with Korean azaleas and ground cover; Little constructed a water wheel of bamboo which adds the melody of falling water to the harmony of wind chimes.

At the west end of the courtyard stands a hexagonal wooden pagoda, assembled by the school's custodial staff. It serves as an outdoor classroom; as an open-air stage for school plays, graduation, and jazz concerts for the local community during Harlem Week; and as a protected playspace for the younger children in inclement weather. As in many European apartment buildings, the

Afro-Asian Friendship Garden.

school's classrooms enclose and overlook the garden courtyard on all four sides. "Harlem," said Cozart, "is the best-known black city in the world. With this Friendship Garden, we are establishing diplomatic ties and beginning a cultural exchange with Japan. The Afro-Asian garden, perhaps the world's first, will be an ever-visible, living symbol to the school children of interracial harmony; and the pagoda, a classroom for cross-cultural study."

Leading from the Center

The gardens vary with their gardeners, manifesting their taste, talent, needs, desires, and budget, but also reflecting Bernadette Cozart's style of leadership. Cozart leads from the center, working *with* — not *for* — community groups and individuals who want a garden. Each time she starts a new garden project, Cozart sits down with the neighborhood or school group who will design, help construct, tend, and own the garden, in order to elicit from them what kind of garden they want. "What's the main purpose of it?" she asks:

To sit and read? Meditate? Grow food?

Beautify a corner? Create a place to meet friends?

Push crack and crime activity out of your block?

What are your favorite colors?

When do you want the garden at its peak?

Do you want scent? Cut flowers?

Viewing from dawn to dusk? A night garden?

A shade garden or full sun?

Water and chimes?

Winding or rectangular paths?

Thus, the design session begins.

One of the first requests to the Coalition for help with a garden came in 1990 from Bishop House, a home for emotionally disturbed women and men. Bishop House had initially paid a contractor thousands of dollars to install a garden; nothing grew in the fill laid over a plastic liner sprayed with herbicides. "Imagine," remarked George Morris, a Greening of Harlem Coalition member, "herbicides in a garden for people who are prescribed medications!" The Coalition was called to rescue the project.

When Cozart asked the Bishop House residents about their preferences for the garden, they asserted that they wanted tranquillity and beauty in their garden. However, the mental health professionals who ran the facility preferred plants for cottage industries, such as herbs and flowers for making potpourri. "I went with the residents," said Cozart emphatically; together they designed a garden with bold and brilliant color, winding walkways, and benches. With two hundred dollars and leftover plants she collected from city agencies and landscape contractors, Cozart designed and built the Bishop House garden with the residents and staff. This backyard refuge, only a few steps from drug-ridden streets, attracted songbirds, hummingbirds, and butterflies. "With a hundred thousand dollars," Cozart later joked, "it could have looked like Paris."

Indigenous Resources

Many young Harlem gardeners are just a few generations removed from the farms and gardens their grandparents cultivated in the Southern United States, Central America, and the Caribbean. "But it takes only two generations to break the cycle of knowledge," says Cozart, who introduces her prospective urban gardeners to the essentials of horticulture. Once they have settled on the kind of garden they want, Cozart pulls out for their perusal four resource guides that she has compiled on plants, planting methods, botany, and insects. (Each winter, when the intensive work of gardens and parks is finished, Cozart scans twenty-five or so horticultural, botany, and entomology publications to update and supplement her guides.) "There's nothing in the planting methods guide I haven't tried," she says, "fruits, vegetables, plant propagation, drying, staking, mulching, soil preparation, and seed storage." Her guide to plant varieties contains many native, non-hybridized species, such as foxglove and bee balm, because they are the hardiest and most disease-resistant plants. Her favorites are plants that give more than one thing to a garden: self-sowers such as cleome;

long-blooming flowers that attract beneficial insects, such as coreopsis; roses for both beauty and scent; liatrus, which dries well; and roadside daylilies, which multiply rapidly and divide easily.

Why does Cozart compile her own insect and botany guides for community gardens? "Hardly any books exist for teachers and kids on insects and botany, so I made my own." There are, she pointed out, no microscopes, and there is no money for educational aids in PS 197 and PS 133, where she designed and planted school gardens with children and teachers. The botany guide contains her own cross-sectional drawings of plants, simplified for the fourth graders of PS 197, with whom she works each winter in the classroom starting seeds, and each spring in their school garden transplanting the seedlings. Their teacher, Joan Weisberger, xeroxes Cozart's botanical drawings for her students to trace and color.

Cozart envisions a flower and vegetable garden, a bird and butterfly garden, a horticultural resource center, and maybe even a greenhouse, in every school in Harlem as "the basis for ecological science in Harlem for adults as well as kids." The key with kids, she said, is to pick plants whose seeds germinate fast, like radishes. "Once the seeds germinate, I've got the kids. Then I teach them

*The garden at
PS 197.*

plant morphology. Kids here are so removed from nature they don't know that just about everything comes from nature—their clothes, their houses, their food."

But she has confidence in both nature and the kids. When she was growing up in Cleveland in the 1950s, every child in her elementary school had a garden, no matter how tiny the plot; teachers would visit the gardens and grade them on their horticulture. Bernadette had planted her backyard garden with vegetables, flowers, and fruit trees by herself because her parents, who had grown up in rural Mississippi and Tennessee, were tired of farming. The abiding taproots that reach back to Cozart's girlhood gardens in Cleveland now sustain the Greening of Harlem: her trust in nature's power to fascinate, her faith in kids' easily stirred curiosity about plants and insects, and her conviction that gardens always give back to their gardeners.

Every Playground Needs a Garden

Dr. Barbara Barlow, a pediatric surgeon at Harlem Hospital, first met Bernadette Cozart in March 1989 at a meeting Barlow called with the Parks Department about the hazardous conditions of the parks in Harlem, Charles Young Park in particular. When the gardener and the surgeon met, Barlow had been chief of pediatric surgery at Harlem Hospital for fifteen years, her first and only surgery post, and director of the Pediatric Trauma Center. She says matter-of-factly, "I will never leave Harlem Hospital." What sets her apart from most surgeons is that she spends more of her time preventing traumatic injuries in children—by lobbying and fundraising for safe playgrounds and parks with gardens and Little League, and by promoting gun safety through schools and clinics—than by putting injured kids back together in the operating room, although she is in the o.r. every morning five days a week and takes night duty every fourth night.

Before 1970, children with gunshot wounds were almost unheard of in Harlem. Between 1970 and 1986, the Harlem Hospital emergency room saw about ten children per year injured by guns, which Barlow linked to kids selling drugs on the street and being given guns by adult dealers. In 1986, with the onset of the crack epidemic, Barlow charted a 300 percent increase in pediatric gunshot wounds, a pattern that continued through 1988 and 1989. She also found that pediatric emergency trauma cases—kids being hit by cars, falling out of apartment windows, being injured in hazardous playgrounds and parks—were on the increase since the mid-1970s, when she had initiated a trauma database to document the cause of injury among children. At one point, Harlem's major injury rate for children was one child in one hundred — ten times the national average. Barlow knew that many of the injuries she was treating in the emergency room were preventable, and in the latter part of the 1970s, she set out to reverse the trend in childhood injuries through education and outreach to the community on injury prevention. In 1988 she formalized and created the Injury Prevention Program.

Her first initiative was to educate parents and pediatricians about the laws regarding installation of window guards. Since that project began in the late 1970s, a majority of apartments in the buildings where children live have been retrofitted with window grates, and the hospital has seen the number of children injured or killed by falling from windows drop from an average of twelve per year to one or fewer. Next Barlow initiated a curriculum in the schools and clinics to educate teens about gun violence; finally, she helped start the Harlem Horizon Art Studio and the Harlem Dance Clinic at the hospital for hundreds of children recuperating from traumatic injuries.

Facing Page: Rubble-strewn lot across the street from PS 133, and the Building Blocks Playground and Garden Project.

The most ambitious and far-reaching of Barlow's injury prevention projects may be the program to restore and return parks and playgrounds — abandoned by the city, haunted by drug dealers, and the refuge of last resort for the homeless — to kids. Like her Coalition partner, Bernadette Cozart, Barlow believes that giving up on parks means giving up on human life. "Concrete doesn't make anyone human, and it certainly doesn't make children human," observed the surgeon.

In 1988 the Robert Wood Johnson Foundation funded the Injury Prevention Program to reduce childhood injuries in Harlem by increasing the number of safe playgrounds and supervised recreational activities. Many Harlem children are confined to their apartments or play on the streets nearby, which explains the many injuries caused by falls and car accidents. The parks and playgrounds, where the children should have been able to play, contained multiple hazards, from broken equipment and metal spikes to rats and drug dealers. To demonstrate the link between the neglect of parks and rising rates of traumatic injury to kids, Barlow hired Theresa Thompkins and Aissatou Bey-Garcia, both lifelong residents of Harlem, to walk through, photograph, and document 120 outdoor play areas operated by the city's public school system, the public housing authority, and the Parks Department.

Thompkins and Bey-Garcia provided firsthand accounts of the contents and condition of Harlem's parks and playgrounds: they were littered with syringes and needles, condoms, rat holes, garbage, mattresses, tables and chairs, old cars, broken concrete, broken metal play equipment, broken glass, broken sewer grates, and non-functioning lights. The homeless and drug pushers inhabited many of these decrepit, dehumanizing neighborhood spaces—the sole public spaces for children and residents of the neighborhood. The two women kept a separate notebook for each play site, which included photographs, descriptions, and documentation, as well as the number of children who had been injured on the playground within the past few months according to records from the Harlem Hospital Emergency Room, outpatient clinics, and school health files. They also recorded their own recommendations for removing the hazards and replacing equipment and play surfaces to make the playgrounds safe for children.

Thompkins and Bey-Garcia identified which organization was responsible for each park and play site—the Board of Education for the school playgrounds, the Department of Parks and Recreation for city parks, and the New York City Housing Authority for recreational areas around public housing projects. Each agency received a letter from Dr. Barlow listing the safety hazards and repairs needed in each park and playground. With the evidence in hand, she began meeting and lobbying with the responsible agencies to get positive action, and sent press releases to local news media to gain publicity and exert public pressure for her safe playgrounds program.

Barlow and her injury prevention staff had begun to investigate bringing Little League baseball back to Harlem when they met Dwight and Iris Raiford, Harlem residents and parents who also wanted to revive Little League after a twenty-year absence from the community. Charles Young Park, with its four ballfields, was the only possibility. After Thompkins and Bey-Garcia documented the state of the park—marked by discarded crack vials, vandalized water fountains, exposed electrical wires, and rat holes—the Harlem Hospital team brought the Parks Department and other city officials together with Dwight and Iris Raiford to present them with their findings.

On the morning of March 29, 1989, *The New York Daily News* ran a story on the hazardous condition of Charles Young Park and the community's plans for reviving Little League in Harlem. That same day, the Parks Department began repairs and replacement of equipment in the park. Later in the spring, Harlem residents, including several men from a nearby homeless shelter, helped remove trash, discarded tires and furniture; the local fire company pitched in, hosing down sidewalks and benches; local police began patrolling the park. Bernadette Cozart oversaw the planting of 150 Betty Prior rose bushes, and the park opened that season for Little League, adult softball, and handball.

On October 29, 1989, the official annual fall community cleanup day for parks throughout the city, more than seven hundred resident volunteers showed up at Charles Young Park to clean, plant bulbs, and watch the unveiling of a mural painted by one hundred local children. Bernadette Cozart supervised kids from the City Volunteer Corps as they planted seven thousand tulip bulbs in the design of an African victory symbol. Recalling the sight of the children planting the tulip garden, Barbara Barlow explained why her work in childhood injury prevention also includes gardens:

> I'm a country person and a garden person and it was so obvious that this was a great activity for kids. I said to Bernadette, "We have to work together so we can help kids learn how to plant gardens." We started working together that day and have never stopped. Every school playground the Injury Prevention Program renovates with safe play equipment and safety surface has to have a garden.

The restoration of Charles Young Park—a waste site of six acres transformed within a few months into the home of the Harlem Little League, an adult softball league, a women's handball association, a rose garden, and an African tulip garden—dramatizes the accomplishments of this almost fail-safe program. Would Charles Young Park ever have been rescued and returned to its community by the Parks Department? Those who have lived with twenty years of municipal neglect of parks and gardens in Harlem say that without the strategic intervention of Harlem Hospital and community groups, many more years would have passed before Harlem's only park with ballfields would have received the investment of capital and resources from the Parks Department.

An Ounce of Prevention

In winter 1992, the Cooper-Hewitt Museum in Manhattan featured an exhibit of maps, among which was a display depicting the results of the Harlem Hospital Injury Prevention Program. Using a software program known as geographic information systems, geographer Cheryl Weisner mapped and compared data on children twelve years and younger who lived in the vicinity of Harlem Hospital and two adjacent hospitals. She color-coded the data to show trends in children's participation in the Harlem Hospital Injury Prevention Programs and numbers of children admitted for injury to Harlem Hospital. The data is compared on the maps with that of two adjacent hospitals in the Washington Heights section of Northern Manhattan and the South Bronx. The first three years of results, from 1988 through 1990, illustrate that as increasing numbers of children participated in the various injury prevention programs of Harlem Hospital, the number of childhood injuries from assault, motor vehicles, outdoor falls, and guns decreased significantly. According to Barlow, more than 2,500 children are now involved in the injury prevention programs, and many more learn safety through outreach programs in the schools. Interestingly, the map indicates that the program's benefits spill over into the Washington Heights neighborhood of Presbyterian Hospital, as almost 30 percent of children participating in the Harlem Hospital Injury Prevention Program were living at that time in Washington Heights. The overall decline in injury rates around Presbyterian Hospital may have to do with the reach of Harlem Hospital's program into Northern Manhattan.

When asked by a reporter whether all of her injury prevention projects— window grates, art, dance, Little League, bicycle helmets, parks, playgrounds, and children's school gardens—is "pediatric medicine," Barlow replied, "What else is it? You're not being killed by being run over by a car, you're not falling off a building, you're not hanging out on a corner where you could be shot." She added with pride, "Harlem is the only part of New York with playground surface made of crumbled tire ground up lighter than cornflakes," referring to the "safety surface" she prescribes for playgrounds.

Edgecomb Avenue Tree-Pit Gardens

On Monday night, November 9, 1992, Lorna Fowler called Barbara Barlow to say that "Jackie Robinson Park looks like Tavern on the Green." Monday evening was the first night in twenty-two years that lights went on in the park. Lorna Fowler watched the park lamps—like a string of large stars festooning an urban forest—from her living room opposite the park on Edgecomb Avenue. Just that morning she had recounted her history of garden, park, and tenant activism to a video crew shooting a film on the Greening of Harlem for the American Institute of Architects. Her block association is a member of the Greening of Harlem Coalition, and she sits on the board.

Edgecomb Avenue is lined on one side by a series of five-story apartment buildings. Lorna Fowler's own building and an adjacent one—both architecturally notable turn-of-the-century buildings—were about to be renovated with

money given by New York City to the tenants' association. Under the guidelines of the grant, when the renovation was finished, the tenants would own and manage their building. Fowler was president of her tenant's association, and she was eager to oversee the installation of new plumbing, heating, and wiring, as well as the plastering and painting.

In the wake of a weak real estate market and numerous tax foreclosures, many absentee landlords abandoned their buildings in Harlem in the 1970s and 1980s, creating a crisis in housing that forced tenants to flee derelict apartments. By the mid-1980s, two-thirds of Harlem's residential buildings were owned, through tax foreclosures, by New York City; whole blocks of brownstones, too costly for the city to repair, are now boarded-up shells of brick and mortar. Some residents turned the crisis of abandonment into an opportunity for tenant ownership and control, and the city of New York made this possible by pioneering an unusual tenant ownership program. Authors Jacqueline Leavitt and Susan Saegert found, in interviews with Harlem tenants who now own their buildings, that the essential ingredient in reversing the tide of neighborhood devastation is "people's care and commitment to place and community."

Leavitt and Saegert also found that the tenants who emerged as leaders in their building were mainly women, often elderly ones, who, like Lorna Fowler, had strong ties with other tenants and great affection for their neighborhood. Leavitt and Saegert attribute these women's skill in managing buildings and organizing tenants to the network of friendship and the informal economy they have traditionally developed in their buildings, neighborhoods, and churches. Years of looking after one another, of keeping an eye on a friend's apartment, or shopping for a sick neighbor, helped build the trust and sense of partnership they needed to take over the ownership and management of their building. Attachment to place—the home in which they have lived for decades, the neighborhood where they know most of their neighbors and where they shop and attend church, and a history-based, memory-laden pride in black Harlem—turned these women into leaders in their buildings when leadership was needed.

Thus it was for Lorna Fowler. Her building and her extended yard in the city—the trees, small gardens, and park on her street—are all of a piece. The side of Edgecomb Avenue opposite her apartment building is lined with mature sycamore trees, a generous sidewalk with benches shaded by the broad canopy of trees, and the tall, gated entrance to Jackie Robinson Park. At the base of each

19

FACING PAGE:
Woman and flowers in tree-pit garden.

tree is a rectangular patch of ground, called a street tree-pit, intended to catch rainwater and permit some decorative plantings. Three years earlier, Fowler cleaned out the weeds and junk that had accumulated in the three-by-five-foot tree-pit across from her apartment. She went into her piggy bank, bought wood, and built a small picket fence around the pit, painted it, and planted flowers. She then talked of taking up a collection in the neighborhood to beautify the tree-pits up and down the block. But her husband said, "You're crazy. No one is going to go for this." However, Fowler's modest gesture of flowers and white picket fence spoke like a sermon to a neighborhood nostalgic for gardens. Her neighbors came to her.

Many seniors who live in the Edgecomb Avenue apartments grew up in rural parts of the South where gardening and farming was a way of life. They longed to put their hands in soil and once again to cultivate flowers and vegetables. Meanwhile, working people on their street wanted their own tree-pit garden; some wanted two. These people were willing to help seniors purchase gardening supplies—one gave as much as $35. Lorna Fowler called the Greening of Harlem for assistance in getting fences, compost and topsoil, seeds and plants. She and Bernadette Cozart contacted the nearby Queensborough Facility to request that inmates in the work-release program help with the gardens. Bernadette trained the men in garden skills, and Lorna set up a system for the inmates to assist seniors in cultivating and caring for their street tree-pit gardens.

Each spring, Lorna and a new group of work-release prisoners clean the pits and repair the white picket and wrought iron fences that frame the gardens. The inmates help the seniors with turning over the soil for planting seedlings, and with watering their gardens, when arthritis or other illness makes it difficult. For seeds and bulbs, soil enriched with leaf mulch, peat moss, manure, and the repair of their fences, the gardeners of Edgecomb Avenue pay Lorna an annual $10 maintenance fee. Thirty-two street tree-pit gardens now line Edgecomb Avenue, between 145th and 155th Streets, and evoke the avenue's erstwhile elegance.

The same day that lights were turned on in the park, Bernadette Cozart came to Edgecomb Avenue with tulip, daffodil, and hyacinth bulbs donated to the Greening of Harlem by the Van Bourgendien bulb company. As she was showing them to Lorna Fowler, ninety-two-year-old Lavinia Jones walked by pushing an upright, wire-framed gardening and shopping cart that supported her as she walked. "Something kept pulling me out," she declared, adding that

Lorna Fowler and Bernadette Cozart visit with a friend at one of the tree-pit gardens.

she came by to get some work-release prisoners to dig the soil around her street tree-pit so she could plant some of the spring flowering bulbs Cozart had provided. "Miss Jones walks down from her fifth-floor apartment three to four times a day to visit her garden," Fowler remarked admiringly, "and her garden is the most beautiful of any." Cozart added, "Seniors' gardens are the best. They may need help digging or repairing fences, but they've got the knowledge. Gardens need knowledge even more than resources."

Cozart especially likes the Edgecomb project because it shows that you can "put gardens anywhere." She and Fowler salvaged plants from roadsides and greenhouses, and collected cobblestones wherever the city was doing road construction, to finish off the street side of the gardens. Old tires, spray-painted an opalescent blue-green and filled with soil, became raised growing beds for marigolds, impatiens, and even peppers and tomatoes. Annual flower seeds—zinnias, marigolds, and asters—are collected by the gardeners in the fall, stored in dark glass jars or envelopes, and then planted the following spring. According to Cozart, they are the only member garden of the Greening of Harlem in which people grow nearly all their plants from seed. In early spring, flats of seedlings fill the windowsills and corners of steps on Edgecomb Avenue, precursors of summer color and beauty that will bring residents out of doors, that will put admiring and vigilant eyes on the street, that will provoke conversation between onlookers and gardeners, that will alchemize a neighborhood into a community.

Jackie Robinson Park

As Lorna Fowler watched miniature gardens around trees transform one block after another, she witnessed simultaneously the demise of nearby Jackie Robinson Park. The main entry to the park across from her apartment building had been boarded up for twenty-two years, ever since the park lights stopped working. People dumped junk cars, mattresses, motorcycles, and sofas into it; the stench was increasing, and, under cover of overgrown trees and bushes, so was drug-dealing and crime. Concerned for the safety of her two daughters, Fowler decided one day in 1991 that she had had enough, and that she wanted to do something about it.

Lorna brought the same organizing acumen she had used to create gardens on Edgecomb Avenue to work on this next and larger challenge. She conferred with Barbara Barlow about the increasing crime in the park, and Barlow had hospital staff begin documenting the number of injuries originating in the park. With Bernadette Cozart she sought approval of the Parks Department and the Queensborough Facility to supervise fifty work-release prisoners from nine to five daily as they removed beds, stoves, and motorcycles, repaired and painted park benches, and painted the Olympic-size pool. Bernadette Cozart taught the prisoners how to prune trees, take down invasive ones, and clear brush, and she arranged for the Department of Public Works to pick up the sorted and piled waste. As they removed weedy saplings and bushes, granite walls capped with concrete suddenly came into view; rays of morning sun could now penetrate and illumine stone walkways. Fowler looked at the bandshell and imagined five thousand tulips—planted under Cozart's direction—blooming the following spring.

Fowler gave each new group of work-release prisoners a half-hour lecture, in English and Spanish, on the dangers of cleaning the park. "Put a stick where you find a needle," she instructed, "and I'll pick it up. Otherwise it will end up in trash bags and someone will get hurt. No hanging out with the dealers, and always wear green shirts in case of a police raid." The first crew she supervised in 1992 helped open up the park; subsequent crews have maintained it under her guidance, doing cleaning, pruning, and painting. The lack of graffiti in the park is no surprise to her: "It's because [the work is] done and maintained by the community." The same lesson of community ownership and community respect has been demonstrated dozens of times in the Greening of Harlem.

Extremely polluted ecosystems are noted for their lack of diversity, supporting fewer species and fewer uses, as they edge toward lifelessness. Likewise, a park, abandoned by its neighbors because it is dull, dangerous, or left by the city to disintegrate, extends its miasma to the local neighborhood. Most think a city poorer without the benefit of parks, writes urban planning critic and commentator Jane Jacobs; but "let us turn this around, and consider city parks deprived places that need the boon of life and appreciation conferred on *them*. A healthy park is one that attracts many people for a diversity of uses at all times of day—to relax after work on a park bench and put aside the din of the day; to stroll by flower gardens; to fly a kite, play on swings, or swim; to seek a tree's shade and privacy with a friend; to attend an evening concert. Cozart graphically described the opening up of an overgrown, dense, dark, and deserted public space, one rife with criminal activity: "Bringing sunshine into Jackie Robinson Park was like spraying a can of Raid in the middle of a room full of cockroaches. They flee in all directions. Where you have positive activity, the negative leaves." The positive activity at this park included a children's garden with coreopsis, daylilies, shrubs, forsythia, tulips, daffodils, and grape muscari, planted by day camp children under Cozart's supervision.

On December 2, 1992, Lorna Fowler led a tour of the newly cleaned, renovated, opened, and lighted Jackie Robinson Park to display the clearing, pruning, and painting that had been done "by the community for the community at no cost to taxpayers" under her supervision. As with the ribbon-cutting ceremony at the greening of Harlem Hospital, the tour was attended by dignitaries

and community leaders, including the Manhattan borough president, Harlem Community Board 9, and local and state politicians. "Before, people didn't even walk down Edgecomb Avenue on the park side. Now," Fowler said with an air of accomplishment, "crime is almost nonexistent," a feat that police and the Parks Department had failed to achieve. Speaking quickly of how sun-filled and alive with people Jackie Robinson Park has become, she called it "her" park, and rightfully so.

Marcus Garvey Park

A few blocks from Edgecomb Avenue and Jackie Robinson Park is Marcus Garvey Park. Originally purchased by the city as an open square in 1839 when Harlem was a sparsely settled farming area, this twenty-two-acre exemplar of Harlem's parks (and Bernadette Cozart's favorite) was ultimately left to disintegrate, to the point that "no children came at all." Marcus Garvey Park, flanked by prominent avenues (Mount Morris Park West and Madison), and adjacent to a historic district, was overtaken by drug dealers and pimps.

In 1990 Ethel Bates, a smart, steely, ebony-skinned woman, got people together to clean the park, removing the same kinds of junk that Lorna Fowler found in Jackie Robinson Park: furniture, old motorcycles, garbage, needles, syringes, and condoms. A year later Bates, whom Cozart calls the "main mover and shaker of Marcus Garvey Park," saw kids playing in the park. Success!

Bates had watched the New York City Parks Department restore other parks, including Fort Tryon Park in Northern Manhattan and Central Park, and she tired of their delay in spending money budgeted for Marcus Garvey Park. She organized the Marcus Garvey Conservancy, a nonprofit organization made up of community members, Harlem politicians, and ministers; and about thirty community groups, including the Greening of Harlem (one of the first to join), the Harlem Hospital Injury Prevention Program, local block associations, schools, and churches. The Conservancy mission statement asserts that:

> the park is sorely in need of upgrading and in its present state is underutilized and taken over by the destructive segments of the community to the exclusion of the general public, particularly the elderly and the children. Everyone should be able to sit on the benches or just stroll around the park in tranquillity. People haven't felt secure in years.

Their objective is to "bring the park back to a well deserved prominence" and "to give an all-encompassing boost to many of our neighbors while paying homage to the memory of Marcus Garvey."

Bates and members of the Conservancy divided the park restoration into five sections according to the geography of the park, and approached community organizations and local businesses to adopt each section. They include: the spacious, flat, shaded grounds that emanate from the base of Mount Morris, a rocky outcrop; the Acropolis, a stone plateau at the tip of Mount Morris overlooking the skyline of Manhattan; the Fire Watchtower, a three-tiered, octagonal, open cast-iron structure that rises with effortless elegance above the Acropolis; the Olympic-size swimming pool and bathhouse; and the Center, a recreational building and outdoor amphitheater. On park clean-up day in spring 1991, when people all over New York City came out to clean up their neighborhood parks, more than six hundred people came to pick up litter, remove graffiti, paint benches, and plant flowers in Marcus Garvey Park. "Of all the five boroughs," boasted Bates, "Harlem had the most volunteers."

In summer 1992, the Conservancy held an evening pool party to "raise awareness, fundraise, and swim under the stars in Harlem." Before the Conservancy started, said Bates, "even police wouldn't patrol parts of the park. Since we started, safety has improved by 90 percent." She predicted that her plan, to have a twenty-four-hour neighborhood security force walking through the park by November 1992, would make Marcus Garvey Park the "only park in New York City where you can come at three o'clock in the morning and be secure."

Bates has a geographer's sense of place and a historian's appetite for lore about the singular, late nineteenth-century architectural character of local late Victorian-style townhouses (once compared favorably with Fifth Avenue mansions), the notable Romanesque Revival churches and the prominent African-Americans who addressed audiences in them, and the park itself. Booker T. Washington spoke at the Ephesus Seventh Day Adventist Church; Marcus Garvey addressed a meeting at the nearby Bethel African Methodist Episcopal Church in 1917 in his campaign to organize the Liberty League. Mount Morris Park was renamed Marcus Garvey Park in 1973.

Bates contends that the park was originally designed by the landscape architect Frederick Law Olmsted, and she wants to see the same quality of restoration put into Marcus Garvey Park that the Parks Department has given to other Olmsted parks, including Central Park and Fort Tryon Park in Manhattan. Yet she is well aware that the downcast park is a metaphor for the people who live near it, and that park restoration must be as connected to their lives as it is to the original landscape design. Like the Greening of Harlem, the Conservancy links the many social needs and problems of the community—AIDS, drugs, hunger, the homeless, seniors, education, and affordable entertainment—with the effort to reclaim the park and restore pride in a once proud and still lingeringly beautiful place.

In 1971 the City of New York designated the area adjacent to the park on the west the Mount Morris Park Historic District. Thus, restoration and repair of the buildings in the district must now conform to the original architectural style. The report supporting the designation traced the district's transition from farmland to a high-fashion suburb of Manhattan which remained a white enclave within black Harlem, until "a great increase in the number of vacancies led to Mount Morris Park's transition to a black neighborhood." Translated this might read: "When whites left the area and no other whites would move in, the market forced desperate landlords to rent to blacks." The writer of the report takes a sort of disembodied delight in the special architectural features of the district, a characteristic which derives from architects' and planners' traditional intellectual detachment of buildings and natural features from the social reality of people who live in and near them.

The "historic district" designation may have preserved the late nineteenth-century Victorian townhouses in the Mount Morris Park section of Harlem from being turned into rooming houses, convenience stores, and community service centers with hodgepodge renovations; but it has not protected Harlem's only large green space, nor the low-income people living in and around the district. What has ensued in the past twenty years, Bates notes, is neglect, decline, and degradation of Marcus Garvey Park, so much so that police refused to patrol the Acropolis. A further irony is the simultaneous disinvestment in low-income housing around Marcus Garvey Park as the historic district was cordoned off for preservation. A recent study on South Central Harlem notes that there has been "a decline in housing units and [consequent] loss in population" around Marcus Garvey Park since 1970, as a result of "reduced federal investment in low-income housing" and the abandonment of apartment buildings by private owners.

What was it about the ailing Marcus Garvey Park that first gripped Ethel Bates and will not relax its hold? She pointed to the original post-and-lintel-

26

framed lookout tower, built to spot fires in Harlem, and elaborated. It was connected by telegraph with the other fire watchtowers in New York so that watchers could use Morse code and signal to each other the whereabouts of a fire. If the fire were in Harlem, the watcher would sound the large alarm bell that hangs from the crossbeam on the second floor of the tower. (Even after fire watchtowers were discontinued in 1878, residents of the Mount Morris area asked the local fire department to sound the bell daily at nine o'clock a.m. and noon.) When Bates first climbed the thirty-nine feet of its slender, spiralling staircase, she "fell in love" with the sweeping 360-degree view of Harlem and beyond. The Fire Watchtower must be saved!

Bates was told that her plan to restore the tower couldn't be undertaken; the tower was too unstable, and the reconstruction would require too much money. The cast-iron tower—the only one of its kind left in New York City, lauded as "absolutely first-rate urban sculpture" and designated a landmark in 1967 by the Landmarks Preservation Commission—was targeted to be dismantled and scrapped. Defiantly, Bates started "bartering, talking, and pulling people in."

"We're churchmouse poor," said Bates, who wrote a grant proposal to the state and won $50,000 to stabilize the tower and keep it from toppling until she could raise money to rebuild it. She had an accountant compute the value of in-kind services from crews of work-release prisoners, the Addict Rehabilitation Center, staunch neighborhood volunteers, and an engineering professor from Columbia University, who evaluated the stability of the fire watchtower. "Thus far," she said in November 1992, "with woman- and manpower, we have put the equivalent of $.5 million into bringing back Marcus Garvey Park." She will not desist until the Acropolis is restored; the stone walls pointed and the capstone repaired; the fire tower renovated; gardens installed and lawns reseeded; benches, children's play areas, and the outdoor amphitheater rebuilt.

What is Bates's secret in talking local artists into teaching dance and drumming, professional acting, chess, and creative writing at the Recreational Center, and in getting stonemasons, carpenters, and local neighborhood people to repair walls and cornices, paint benches, and seed acres of lawns? "I'm a pushy woman," she explained. "The Coalition is full of pushy women," rejoined Bernadette Cozart.

Looking out from the top of Mount Morris to the Manhattan skyline and the mouth of the Harlem River where it joins the East River, the two women conjured up the park's future. "Someday there will be concerts on the Acropolis,"

said one. The other gestured to where gardens designed by the Greening of Harlem will animate the gray granite surface and stone block walls with their bright, variegated, sweeping color and texture, and curvaceous lines. Playgrounds and play areas evaluated by the Harlem Hospital Childhood Injury Prevention Program for their hazards will be restored with the playground safety surface and equipment that have become the hallmark of that program. "Marcus Garvey Park," said Cozart, "could easily be the flagship park of the community, if not the borough."

From a Three-Piece Suit to Coveralls

As a teenager, George Morris went to concerts at the bandshell in Jackie Robinson Park, and watched exhibition basketball in Charles Young Park. He helped host the evening pool party at Marcus Garvey Park in the summer of 1992. "In Harlem, *parks and recreation* is an oxymoron" he said candidly. "Before the Greening of Harlem, you could count on your hands the number of healthy trees in parks. As for recreation, there was none." The Parks Department program functioned "like Plessy vs. Ferguson, separate but equal," and Harlem got the Parks workers with the poorest performance records and broken equipment.

Morris met Cozart and Barlow on a bus tour of Harlem parks in 1989 organized by Barlow's Childhood Injury Prevention Program. While touring the parks, Cozart, who was sent by her boss at the Parks Department, explained the tree and shrub species to the group. George Morris was impressed by Cozart's knowledge, and by the extent of the community organizing on behalf of the Greening of Harlem Coalition that he was witnessing on the bus tour. At the time, he was Director of Volunteers and Community Liaison for the Manhattan Borough of Parks and Recreation. He promoted Department of Parks and Recreation projects "in a three-piece suit" by bringing community groups together and organizing volunteers for the annual spring and fall cleanups in city parks. By 1990, he was working in Marcus Garvey Park "in coveralls" as the Parks Department community liaison for the Greening of Harlem. He found a van for the Coalition, which saved Bernadette Cozart from having to transport tools and garden supplies for projects all over Harlem. As community liaison, Morris received calls from people and groups who wanted help from the Greening of Harlem to start a community garden. His first call was from Lorna Fowler when she started to organize the street tree-pit gardens on Edgecomb Avenue.

A typical work day with the Greening of Harlem began with following up on a call, like the one from Lorna, about starting a garden. Some callers thought the Coalition was a poverty agency that would come and put the garden in for them. Morris set them straight right away: "You do the garden; the Greening of Harlem will show you how." Next he looked at the neighborhood space, assessed the possibilities for a community garden, and set up a meeting with himself, Bernadette Cozart, and the person or group on site. At the meeting Bernadette worked with the group to discern the kind of garden that they wanted, how much experience they had with gardens, whether they wanted a high- or low-maintenance garden, and so on. She discussed what the group's responsibilities for the garden were, and began the design session with them. George became the Coalition's factotum and helped wherever needed: picking up plants at the Parks Department's greenhouses; hauling cow manure from a farm in North Jersey; working in the gardens with the community gardeners; attending community meetings in the evening; making press and other media contacts; doing an interview on a local radio station.

FACING PAGE:
Passer-by looking through fence into PS 133 garden.

"The Greening of Harlem is not a 'give you' program like some other green-ing and open space programs that put in cookie-cutter gardens or make exorbi-tant amounts of money as another ghetto-pimp program," he said emphatically. "It is built on tapping people's talents and empowering people." He illustrated his point with the pool party under the stars at Marcus Garvey Park: A jazz combo played, Lorna Fowler (also a professional caterer) sold food, and every-body learned about the community plans for the revival of the park. "Manhattan parks have few volunteers," he said. "Harlem has more volunteers than all the other parks in Manhattan combined." The Coalition has a different kind of power and wealth, Morris explained, based on an alternative economy in which each person gives of their talents and networks with community organizations and agencies to get equipment, seeds, and plants. "The more that has been taken away from us, the more we got because we became more self-reliant and resourceful."

Asked about the "best scenario" for the Greening of Harlem, Morris laid out the ideal conditions as he saw them. First, it would be a community organiza-tion, outside of government. It would have the infrastructure it currently lacks: an office, a greenhouse, a van, gardening supplies, a computer with computer-aided design functions, paid staff with gardeners, an herbalist, and a nutritionist. There would be theme gardens: gardens for Vietnam vets, for people with AIDS, and for pregnant and parenting teens. Cottage industries would spring up — grasses and bamboo would be grown for basket weaving, and gardeners would sell their wares from herb and garden carts on Harlem street corners.

The Greening of Harlem is "everybody's story" he concluded. It's the story of seniors from the Edgecomb street tree-pit gardens who show fourth graders at PS 197 how to make "cha cha" with the hot peppers from their school garden, and tell them about methods of food preservation before refrigeration. It's the story of the emotionally troubled woman at Bishop House who explained that she loves to work in the garden there every day because the plants need her. It's the story of nine fourteen-year-old blacks and Latinos learning horticulture, self-respect, thrift, and humanism from a black woman gardener who made them deal with their machismo while she taught them how to lop tree branches. "We're negating everything, sexism, racism, classism — all of the negatives — and working with pregnant teens, people with emotional problems, drug prob-lems, AIDS . . . in doing these gardens. What exists — the gardens, the momen-tum, the funding sources, and the people of good will — should not be lost."

Part of Something Larger

For Bernadette Cozart, the local in the Greening of Harlem reveals the universal. "Children growing up in Harlem have never known nature . . . Gardens teach us that we are part of something much larger—redwoods, whales, and rainforest."

She moves on seamlessly to the local economic potential.

> I've got this land reclamation thing in my head. When I look at Harlem, I see a community ready to burst forth. I see vacant lots as sources of jobs. I can see growing vegetables and herbs and going all the way from seed to shelf. In specialty shops, you see all kinds of delicacies. I envision watermelon rind jelly, tomato preserve, and "cha cha" with labels that say "grown and made in Harlem." Many people in the community grew up in the South. Traditions like canning were left but not lost. I can see making dyes and potpourries, raising herbs for healing and culinary uses. I can see a vineyard right here in Harlem. . . . Why not? . . . And grapes, fermented and bottled into Harlem *Champagne*.

> Those of us in the Greening of Harlem see Harlem in a positive light. We see the potential of Harlem. I view Harlem as my living room. How will we want our living room to look? . . . Look at the buildings and structures here—they're gorgeous. Add the beauty of nature to Harlem and give kids who have only known New York City as concrete and steel the chance to get to know nature. . . . We have to figure out a way to bring nature to the city.

As for the future, Cozart envisions the Greening of Newark, the Greening of New Brunswick, the greening of every city that suffers the same disasters as Harlem: abandoned and run-down buildings, vacant lots, illegal dumping of trash and chemicals, drugs, crime, violence, homelessness, malnutrition, and all the human problems that result from such inhumane living conditions. Her vision of moving Harlem into the twenty-first century involves turning vacant lots to small farms, tree and shrub nurseries, flowering gardens, herb gardens, and playgrounds. She sees abandoned, city-owned buildings—of which there are hundreds in Harlem—converted into woodworking or carpentry shops,

"Look at the buildings and structures here—they're gorgeous. Add the beauty of nature to Harlem . . ."

blacksmith shops, and glassblowing factories. A variety of products—wrought iron work, glassware, quilts, specialty foods, crafts, cosmetics, and champagne from the first African-American vineyard—would be sold by mail order to retailers and to the community. Carpenters would renovate community housing ("open space also includes vacant buildings"). Block by block the community would be restored, made beautiful, and employed.

Once, when asked by a foundation interested in funding the Greening of Harlem to define the boundaries of her community, Cozart replied, "Eighty-fourth Street to Yonkers." Laughing at the sudden expansion of Harlem's borders north and south, she added: "Actually, Harlem stretches from ghettos here to shantytowns in Soweto. Harlem is global; it is replicated worldwide on every continent and in every race. And it's *women*. There have been many holocausts of women, but we are waking up."

Riverbank State Park

On May 28, 1993, *The New York Times* carried a story about a new state park in Harlem: "A Park, However It Smells, Blossoms on the River." Riverbank State Park—twenty-eight acres of athletic facilities, picnic areas, a restaurant, an amphitheater, and walking paths atop the North River Water Pollution Control

Plant overlooking the Hudson River—is West Harlem's *compensation* for being burdened and blighted by the North River sewage treatment plant.

On opening day "it simply stunk," the columnist wrote. Sixty-five-year-old Lillie Elliot, who lives several blocks from the plant, came to the grand opening to see what authorities were planning to do about the sewage smell that has plagued her apartment since the plant opened seven years ago. While school-children romped and had picnics with teachers, several members of the West Harlem Environmental Action (WHEACt) stood at the park's entrance at 145th Street and Riverside Drive with placards and petitions. The environmental coalition had sued the City of New York on behalf of the community and, as part of their demands, wanted the government to study the long-term health impacts of the sewage treatment plant's air emissions on children who play at the park. WHEACt, according to founding member Vernice Miller, is one of the good seeds sown that has taken root in the West Harlem community's thirty-year struggle against the siting of the North River plant.

On March 28, 1962, the New York City Planning Commission met in a closed hearing and voted to change the planned location of the North River sewage treatment plant from the Upper West Side of Manhattan between West 70th and West 72nd Streets, to West Harlem between 137th and 145th Streets.

From the early 1960s onward district and borough politicians, including the district leader David Dinkins, mobilized residents of West Harlem who were overwhelmingly opposed to a plant that would treat the waste of nearly one million people (170 million gallons per day) in their backyard. "These are the indignities that make people feel they are not equal," Percy Sutton, the only black representative on the Board of Assessors, testified at a hearing in which the board voted to appropriate funding for constructing the plant. The plant has malfunctioned since it opened in 1986, fouling the air of a residential Harlem neighborhood, and it has obliterated their view of the Hudson River. The offensiveness of the sewage plant became the community's bitter bargaining chip for a first-class recreational park, a public resource that Harlem has historically been denied.

The current plight of West Harlem—damned with and damned without the Riverbank State Park—is the legacy of Robert Moses, the domineering master planner of New York City for thirty years. During the 1930s, as Commissioner of the New York City Department of Parks and Recreation, Moses built 255 playgrounds in the city. Only one was built in Harlem, where two hundred thousand children were playing in streets, alleys, and abandoned vacant lots littered with broken glass, dog feces, and garbage. His inaction in the 1930s exacerbated a series of social conditions—including higher rents and lower wages than the rest of the city, crowded schools, and congested, neglected, unsanitary buildings—that turned the largest and most concentrated black city of the world into the worst slum in New York City. In 1950, the *Times* did an investigative piece on playgrounds for Harlem children and reported "bare-legged children" played "on dumps of broken glass, rusty cans, and refuse." Throughout the 1980s, Dr. Barbara Barlow operated on children at Harlem Hospital who were injured on broken equipment in decadent playgrounds and on the streets because parks were neglected, derelict, and the site of drug dealing.

According to Moses's biographer Robert Caro, in building his monumental state parks and parkways as State Commissioner of Parks, Moses had no interest in building for the lower classes. He located new parks remote from the poor, particularly people of color, and ensured by low bridge clearances that only cars—then a luxury of the middle and upper middle class—could use the parkways. Then as New York City Parks Commissioner, he cheated the people of Harlem out of their section of the six-mile-long Riverside Park, the signature piece of his West Side Improvement. All major investment, improvements, and amenities in Riverside Park stopped at 125th Street, the border of Harlem. Vernice Miller, a resident of West Harlem and a major voice calling for environmental justice in her community, sums up the double standard in municipal park policy that left Harlem vulnerable to further environmental insult:

> Robert Moses spent millions of dollars enlarging Riverside Park, but he spent absolutely nothing between 125th and 155th streets. He added 132 acres to Riverside Park in white neighborhoods, but not one acre was added to the portion of the park in Harlem where black people lived. In effect, the Harlem section of Riverside Park was no park at all, much as it remains today. Robert Moses condemned and removed all commercial developments from the waterfront along the portion of Riverside Park running south of 125th Street, yet the Harlem waterfront was covered with commercial and industrial uses; they were allowed to remain on what would otherwise have been waterfront parkland. This too remains unchanged today.

With this "Mason-Dixon line" policy for West Harlem's riverside in the late 1930s, Moses set the stage for the New York City Planning Commission to select the riverfront in Harlem as the site for West Manhattan's wastewater treatment plant. The compensatory Riverbank State Park is now welcomed — it was visited by an average of ten thousand people per day in its first month — only because it is desperately needed.

While depriving Harlem of grand parks and barring the poor from state parks and the best of city parks by banning public transportation to them, Moses might have at least given crumbs from the master's table — vest-pocket parks, one- to three-lot parks for sitting, playing, and some morsel of green and garden. But he quickly lost interest in turning vacant, city-owned lots in slums into parks and playgrounds: too much red tape, too small-scale for public notice, too expensive an investment for the return, not enough reflected glory. Consequently, in an entire three square miles of Harlem in the 1930s, where three hundred thousand people lived, "there wasn't a single patch of green." Within a decade Mount Morris Park, later Marcus Garvey Park, would inadvertently proffer a small oasis of green to people of color, as black people, and therefore, the boundary of Harlem, pushed south from 125th Street.

A recent study of New York City parkland reveals the lasting consequences of a public policy in which parks and public gardens were deemed the entitlement of the white well-off. The study shows "that race and income are significantly correlated to the distribution and quantity of parkland per capita by community district." The amount of parkland available to people "decreases as median income decreases and as the proportion of residents of color increases." Further, of the new parkland acquired by the Parks Department in the 1980s (530 acres), 95 percent was in wealthier, white districts that already enjoyed more parkland than underserved districts. The study concludes that strategies to increase open space in New York City must focus on low-income communities of color: "While these communities are not replete with wetlands and other natural areas, they do have an abundance of another resource—vacant land—that could be transformed into parkland."

The communities that lack parks and gardens because of decades-old neglect are the same ones that now have a surplus of vacant land because of decades of economic disinvestment. Central Harlem alone has 662 vacant lots—one out of every eight lots—the equivalent of 112 acres. Looking at any one of them, Bernadette Cozart gets "this land reclamation thing" in her head.

Bernadette Cozart and Fred Little in the Afro-Asian Friendship Garden before the planting.

Can a "bunch of pushy women" undo the damage of a sixty-year legacy of land use planning that forces Harlem residents to resort to abandoned lots and buildings and a sewage treatment plant for community gardens, parks, and open space? Four elements, in particular, contribute to the resiliency, the already remarkable achievements on a shoestring budget, and the potential of the Greening of Harlem to correct a few of history's wrongs. They are: the model of organization; anchored gardens; available land; and a vision steeped in the spirit of place.

The Greening of Harlem is a circular chain of individuals and institutions in which each link is unique, relies on the others, but also works from its own center of strength. Barbara Barlow, with institutional savvy and a persistent pragmatism, brought city institutions together—School Board with Hospital, Parks Department with Hospital—when all the homework was done on playground and park hazards and related childhood injuries. She uses the press skillfully to hold public agencies accountable for their recreational facilities in Harlem. Lorna Fowler is an eminent manager—of people, of buildings, of budgets, of the large- and small-scale, from tree-pits to parks. Her acute sense of home and domestic economy extends generously from her cooperatively-owned building, to her street and neighbors, to "her" park. Ethel Bates has a single-minded, intelligent passion for the history of place, the geography of place; her pushy civic pride, her relentless research, organizing, and fundraising, will put Marcus Garvey Park back on the map of significant New York City parks. Bernadette Cozart will reverse Robert Moses's writeoff of Harlem as unworthy of gardens and parks: Her spirit matches his ego; her humanistic horizons surpass his self-interested ones. Moses took people out of the city to "his" grand parks on a network of highways that was built on the detritus of neighborhoods he disdained; Cozart restores humans and the environment of Harlem with a profound love for both.

Community gardens everywhere in the United States have fragile tenure, often because the land being gardened is not owned or leased long-term by the gardeners, but sometimes because the gardeners do not sustain interest in the garden. The community gardens of the Greening of Harlem are moored to (and thus secured by) institutions and community organizations: Harlem Hospital, PS 133, 92, and 197, the School for Pregnant Teens, Edgecomb Avenue Security Block Association, Marcus Garvey Park, the Upper Room AIDS Ministry, and so on. Children's murals in gardens and parks everywhere express their sense of

pride and identification with Harlem, an intangible that further binds gardeners with their gardens. The Greening makes one believe that every abandoned
lot is waiting for a new Harlem Renaissance that will reunite nature with vibrant
human life. The expanded sense of environment here—the human, the architectural, the natural, the ethical—enriches and adds complexity to this more-
than-a-greenspace program. As George Morris urged, "What exists—the gardens, the momentum, the funding sources, and the people of good will—

38

SAN FRANCISCO:
A Class of Stars

PREVIOUS PAGE:
*Hunter's Point
gardeners.*

In 1982 Cathrine Sneed, a counselor at the San Francisco County Jail in San Bruno, set out to teach inmates how to grow vegetables and flowers in a novel eight-acre classroom called the Horticulture Project. She was prompted to do this by a brush with a life-threatening illness. Today she is special assistant to the sheriff and director of the Garden Project, a half-acre organic market garden and community service program in San Francisco, which she founded in 1991 for "graduates" of the Horticulture Project.

The law-and-order, tough-on-the-criminal Lieutenant Robert Limacher, "wasn't sure about a garden project" when Sneed first started; but today he is convinced. Limacher, who oversees the day-to-day operations at the jail and the eight-acre garden, described traditional county jails as "bars and steel institutions where inmates and even employees become devalued and hardened. It's almost insurmountable when people come to jail; most have nothing. People don't learn shit in prison." He added that jails don't prevent crime, prisons don't rehabilitate, and recidivism is very high; but "the Horticulture Project instills a sense of value about themselves in inmates." He contrasted students in the garden project with other inmates: "They don't have the institutionalized jail mind. They develop more self-awareness and are more willing to hold themselves accountable for what they did and what they don't want to repeat."

Crime prevention is Lieutenant Limacher's bottom line. Teaching students to "take the garbage out of their life and make it something they can grow from" is horticulture instructor Arlene Hamilton's unremitting mission. In her classroom each part of plant and soil life becomes a teaching point for her students' lives. One of her favorite metaphors is compost: Every troubled spot, every yellow leaf, can be turned back into productive soil. So, too, with the lives of her students.

On a Monday morning in late March 1994, Arlene Hamilton called her new class of more than two dozen men to attention to discuss the jobs they could sign up for in the horticulture class:

Kitchen: We need two people for the kitchen. They must be diplomats. Some people get into a power trip with food.

Greenhouse: five students can work with seedlings. This job requires much care and *focus* (one hears that word often) on planting seeds and thinning and watering seedlings.

Harvest: Six people can pick, clean, remove yellow leaves, and package. We send the best food we grow. This year we have already grown sixty thousand pounds here for the homeless. Food is not charity, it's justice. Food is a human right.

Weeding: We need fifteen people for weeding. What does weeding symbolize? Clearing out problems—so plants can grow the best they can. Your life is like that plant: you need to get the weeds out.

Compost: A couple of students are needed to add waste material to the compost pile and turn it over. Compost helps us to be organic gardeners. And it's a symbol of turning mistakes into lessons.

Tree Crew: Students are needed to weed around trees that earlier students planted.

Bed Preparation: This is the most important job. Ten men prepare the beds where seedlings will be transplanted. It's like having a home to come to.

Hamilton ended the hour-long class with a challenge. "I notice that some of my students are back. In this program we are focusing on *job preparation.* When you leave the Horticulture Project here, Cathrine Sneed has the Garden Project for you next."

Hamilton met her second class of men in the greenhouse—a color-filled, graceful, and airy home to thousands of seedlings, which was designed by environmental artist Ned Kahn in collaboration with Cathrine Sneed. (Kahn had been commissioned to create a piece of art for the jail and on talking with Sneed and seeing the organic garden at San Bruno, he decided to produce a work for the Horticulture Project. Dichroic (two-colored) glass panels placed in parts of the greenhouse infuse the space with vivid cobalt blue, yellow gold, and other combinations of color. "A greenhouse can be art, and art can feed the homeless," Kahn said about the collaboration.) In the greenhouse, Arlene held a brief discussion of work details before heading out to the gardens. The day's tasks were to continue raised bed preparation and to begin transplanting romaine lettuce seedlings.

After an hour in the field, everyone gathered again for discussion in a large open room in the barn. The walls display pictures of Sojourner Truth, Martin Luther King, and Gandhi, interspersed with posters that read: "Silence is death," "People need water not weapons," and "Save the Rainforest." An invitation was posed to the class: "If the garden has helped you in any way, please tell us." The students took turns telling what the garden meant to them, while a bilingual student translated into English or Spanish and Arlene intermittently offered her comments:

"It gives me responsibility and unity."

"It gets us out of the city."

"And brings us closer to nature." (Arlene)

"The garden helps us to focus."

"I like the chemical-free food." (This student has picked some greens for cooking).

"I learn respect for life."

"Don't step on the spinach beds, gentlemen," their teacher chided and reminded. The interpreter added first in English and then Spanish: "For people who did walk through the beds that José and I put in, it really hurt me." "Did they apologize?" Arlene asked. "One did."

"Gardens teach me self-control."

"If you can take this lesson with you, gentlemen, you won't be back." (Arlene)

"I get peace of mind."

"Families are like gardens," Arlene interjected. *"Honor their lives—care for women and care for children—like you do the plants."*

"I like it because I see a beginning and an end. You put it in, see it grow, and harvest it."

Arlene illustrated how some good deeds linger after them: "One student is leaving jail in a few days. He had planted spinach seeds that are now seedlings. When they grow and are harvested, his good work will still be going on."

"It gives me a good feeling and I get relaxed."

One student introduced himself as Clayton:
"This is only my first day. In the garden you work with a variety of cultures and it teaches you to do that in society."

Arlene closed the class by asking students who were leaving jail soon to speak to the class on Thursday about *preparing for freedom* and *maintaining your freedom*.

That afternoon a third horticulture class of fifteen to twenty women gathered in the greenhouse. While Arlene explained the work assignments—planting the remaining romaine lettuce seedlings in new beds prepared by the morning class, watering the seedlings, and weeding the beds—one student, Nina, broke off yellow leaves from kale seedlings as carefully and naturally as if they were her own houseplants. Arlene took the women to the newly prepared raised beds and demonstrated how one student could make a narrow trench with the edge of a hoe and two others could follow to plant the romaine lettuce seedlings. She explained how to plant in parallel rows across the wide bed, placing four transplants in one row and five in another, spaced diagonally to give the plants more growth area.

Arlene pointed to a weak, spindly seedling. "Like some of my students, sometimes they don't look too strong either; but in time they grow and get healthy like this plant will." She encouraged students to hill more soil around new young transplants that need more support with the maxim: *gardening is trust*. "Three seconds for each plant," she called to another with a watering can who followed those planting. "Just like reporting to parole, you need to keep it up and not miss one time." And to those weeding, "Weeds are like pimps and drug dealers. If you let them take root, they'll strangle you." She added quickly, "How does it feel to do something good for the people—even in jail? Your food goes to soup kitchens that feed three thousand people per week." A sequence of rapid replies from those planting, watering, and weeding followed her question—"energy from the sun," "good compost and good soil," "fresh air," "positive thinking—it's all good." Arlene pointed out a red-tailed hawk and its young circling and soaring above the farm. Someone started singing and others joined her, "I'm gonna fly like an eagle to the sea, fly like an eagle, let me fly like an eagle, let my spirit carry me."

Coming back reluctantly from planting when their hour in the field was up, women pointed to clumps of herbs they use for tea—lemon balm, chamomile, catnip, peppermint—and compared herbal remedies for cramps and insomnia. Some harvested kale leaves and grabbed bulbs of garlic for cooking that evening. The air clears the mind, said a student named Renita, who would work all day in the garden, and even have her lunch there, if she could.

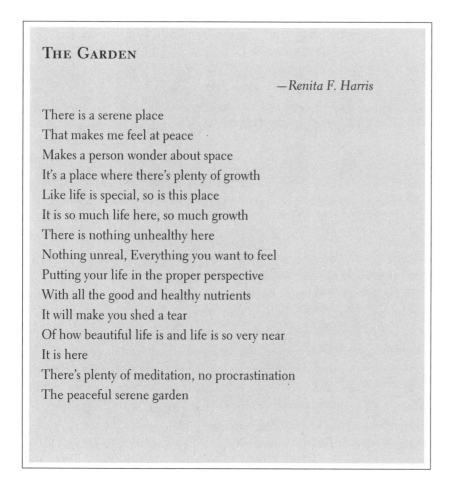

THE GARDEN

—Renita F. Harris

There is a serene place
That makes me feel at peace
Makes a person wonder about space
It's a place where there's plenty of growth
Like life is special, so is this place
It is so much life here, so much growth
There is nothing unhealthy here
Nothing unreal, Everything you want to feel
Putting your life in the proper perspective
With all the good and healthy nutrients
It will make you shed a tear
Of how beautiful life is and life is so very near
It is here
There's plenty of meditation, no procrastination
The peaceful serene garden

The Decline of Schools and the Rise of Prisons

As a community, we must address the adverse life circumstances that spawn criminality. These things are not quick and they're not easy, but they're effective.

—Wilbert Rideau, Inmate
Editor, *Angolite*, Louisiana State Penitentiary

Most of the nearly four hundred inmates in San Bruno are there for a misdemeanor conviction, usually a drug-related offense. Even most of those charged with burglary and assault, according to Limacher, are also involved in illegal drug activity. Their sentence of one year or less translates into little more than five months at San Bruno. "By the time Arlene Hamilton gets them, they have two to three months left, that's all the time she has to work with them."

He credits Michael Marcum, director of the jail's Program Facility, with the many educational and skills programs at San Bruno. Marcum has pioneered this model of "new generation" jail based on custody, respect for the individual, and an intensive offering of life and vocational skills classes and programs. About twenty programs are available for inmates, ranging from GED, ESL, literacy, tutoring, video production, and auto mechanics, to classes on parenting and domestic violence, twelve-step groups, creative writing, drama, and horticulture. The physical facility expresses as well this philosophy of respectful supervision and individual responsibility. Bars have been replaced with walls, doors, and glass; groups live in a common pod where they sleep, have class, and cook. The men and women who live in pods and participate in the skills programs have signed an agreement that forbids violence, drugs and alcohol, and verbal expressions of racism and sexism.

Pressed about what makes the Horticulture Project effective for inmates in such a brief period of time—two to three months, on average—Limacher observed that horticulture is the most "humanistic" of all the programs, even more so than Alcoholics Anonymous, drug, and cultural value group sessions. "Getting outside into fresh air every day and the measure of trust that Hamilton and her staff build are effective at breaking down the criminal mentality of 'I'm here because police put me here' to 'I'm here because of dealing in drugs.'" He cites the effectiveness of the "powerful metaphors" that the instructors use, "for instance, organic gardening is like a chemical-free body and a cleansing of the mind." Limacher added as an afterthought how critical it is that the food the prisoners grow goes to soup kitchens and programs for the homeless in San Francisco: "This too gives a clean feeling of self-respect." Traditionally, city jails have been run like businesses, using the free labor of the inmates; food grown on jail farms, for instance, was used in the jail kitchen. Limacher feels that it devalues programs to set them up to make money from the work of inmates, and that it degrades the inmates.

Prisons are being built in California at a rate faster than the state can make them operational; completed facilities stand empty, and existing facilities are overcrowded. Two authors rank California, which houses one out of every eight prisoners in the United States, as "the world's largest and most crowded prison system." The National Center on Institutions and Alternatives calculated that in 1989 per capita spending on "criminal justice" was $130, while $106 was spent per capita on education. One commentator attributes the decline of the state college and university system in California to the expansion of its prison system.

The "war on drugs"—wherein drug use is treated primarily as a criminal justice issue rather than as a social failure and personal crisis—has resulted in the extraordinary growth in prison and jail populations beginning in the 1980s, and in what Angela Davis calls "the ideological merging of racialization and criminalization." In San Francisco, 60 percent of all inmates were sentenced for drug- or alcohol-related charges. The figure rises to nearly 85 percent when inmates are included who had drug charges dropped before sentencing. Of those in jail, most are poor and people of color: African-Americans constitute 50 percent of the San Francisco jail population, while they make up only 9 percent of the city's population. A study by the National Institute of Drug Abuse found that African-Americans constitute only about 12 percent of those who use drugs regularly, yet more than 36 percent of those arrested for drug violations are black.

Many, if not most, prison inmates probably did not finish high school, and lack job skills and the confidence to apply for a job; they also may not be able to read job application forms. Many, especially women, were physically and sexually abused as children, and this abuse lies at the root of their prostitution and drug use. An oral history project conducted by WHISPER (Women Hurt in Systems of Prostitution Engaged in Revolt) found that 90 percent of prostituted women interviewed had been subjected to an "inordinate amount of physical and sexual abuse during childhood." For many, the only way to end violence is to run away from home. Young, unable to get a job or find shelter, they "are easy prey for pimps." Seventy percent reported being beaten by pimps; 74 percent were assaulted by tricks. (Why are prostitutes and not the pimps and johns the primary targets of arrest?) Yet, a 1989 survey of 1,700 jails reported that only 7 percent provided a range of services including drug education and planning for the transition from and after jail.

Sheriff Michael Hennessey oversees county jails in San Francisco, where the number of inmates has tripled since 1970, and which are consequently filled to capacity. He, too, regards the Horticulture Project at San Bruno and the Garden Project for post-release inmates on Carroll Street in San Francisco eminent crime prevention programs. Simply warehousing criminals in jail cells and then releasing them, using jails as a quick-fix punishment for crime or drug use, only creates what Hennessey calls a "criminal justice turnstile." Even the typical job skills and job placement programs in and after jail don't provide the social services that are needed by most inmates. The horticulture projects, he feels, do.

Hennessey doesn't have the time or funds to undertake a recidivism study; but years of watching jails harden people who could have turned their lives around have convinced him that the farming, gardening, and tree planting projects help motivate people, build their self-esteem, and save them from

Young women and flowers at the Hunter's Point Garden.

turning back to crime and the streets. With or without a study, Hennessey is sure that the gardening program has enabled more people to get themselves out of the recurrent loop of crime because he has seen up close the change it has made in individual inmates and former inmates.

His staff agreed. Lieutenant Rebecca Benoit, who manages the county jail in San Bruno, corroborated Hennessey's evaluation with her day-to-day observations of the almost immediate effect that participation in the Horticulture Project has on new inmates. "People come in here with their hands in their pockets, looking down, full of attitude," she observed. Once they get started weeding and working in the garden, "they're clear-eyed, they're saying hello every morning to the staff and the counselors and to each other. It's really very amazing."

Life Literacy

Cathrine Sneed points to a handful of books that convinced her she could teach life skills to people in jail using the garden as a classroom, and organic agriculture as a course in insight, focus and discipline, and even love. One was Jonathan Kozol's *Death at an Early Age*, an exposé of inner-city Boston public schools, where she saw the school experiences of many of her own students at San Bruno in Kozol's descriptions of the children he had taught.

In October 1964 Jonathan Kozol began substitute teaching in a de facto segregated fourth-grade classroom of a Boston public school. The "classroom" was a corner of an auditorium where other classes were also being held; a large window fell in during class in winter, and months went by before it was properly fixed; other children attended class in a "dark and dusty and urine-smelling cellar." Kozol wrote of teachers calling the African-American students "animals" and their school building "a zoo." Whippings across the fingers with a rattan were frequent; no traffic officer could be gotten to guide children across a major avenue. Kozol described white male teachers as finding "masculine fortification" in whipping and humiliating black children. The emblematic child he fictionalized as Stephen might well be some of the many young black men in prison today; another, Angelina, could be any one of the women whose prime safety net is Cathrine Sneed's Garden Project.

Stephen, at eight years old, had poor math and reading skills. He was beaten by a foster mother and had had mainly a series of substitute teachers. Kozol recognized that Stephen had a talent for art, the expressionist kind that will not respect straight lines; yet the rigid, rulebound art teacher tore up his work and dropped it in a waste basket in front of the class. Stephen was odd at times, withdrawn, and eccentric; and for this he was beaten on the hands by teachers and later that year was sent to a home for the emotionally disturbed. Kozol, however, found him an "indescribably" gentle and "non-malicious" child.

Angelina was also talented in art. Not docile or passive, she was disliked by teachers for having a mind of her own—an asset they interpreted as insolence and surliness. Kozol had planned to help enroll Angelina in a summer art class for children at the museum school, but before he could, he was fired from his job for using a Langston Hughes poem in class about a neglectful white landlord and an outspoken black tenant.

In a 1985 epilogue to his 1967 book, Kozol tells the fate of the children whose minds were pulverized, whose spark was snuffed out in the Roxbury public school. In 1983 Stephen knifed and killed a man who called him "an illiterate subhuman." Angelina had three children and was living on welfare. She could not read the newspaper, or advertisements for jobs, or fill out forms for welfare or for jobs; nor could she read her children's homework. She could be any one of the women in San Bruno County jail driven to selling drugs, grand larceny, or prostitution, because she was unprepared to do much else.

FACING PAGE:
Group portrait
after
community
service.

A society that invests $106 per capita in schools while spending $130 per capita on prisons and jails dooms itself to more crime, as it augments the criminal landscape in which larger and larger numbers of its members live, and to which they return worsened by jail and prison culture. Kozol estimates that one-third of adult Americans—sixty million people—are basically illiterate. Of these, twenty-five million can't even read poison warnings on a can of pesticide, nor can they read a letter from their child's teacher or a job notice in a newspaper. The United States ranks forty-ninth in literacy among 158 member countries of the United Nations, and only 4 percent of the illiterate American population is reached by federal, state, and private literacy programs. Where children do stay in school, schools in poor districts may only be able to invest in each child one-quarter to one-third of the resources available to children in the wealthiest school districts.

Yet even if her students learned to read job notices and letters from their child's teacher, Cathrine Sneed knew that print literacy would not be enough. They needed life literacy.

The Garden Project

At 10:00 a.m. on Tuesday, March 22, 1994, class in the Garden Project began with a fifteen-minute exercise session outdoors conducted by a man named Demetrius, who moved the students from head rolls and touching their toes to arm rolls, jump rope, jumping jacks, and a warm-down with a few dance steps in place. The session included lots of counting in chorus, lots of fast-moving instruction, and lots of fun—but serious fun, fun that's focused, disciplined, and healthy, like the rest of the Garden Project. Next came a breakfast of fruit, juice, coffee, and muffins, served cafeteria-style inside a spacious, ground-floor classroom on the Southeast Campus of the City College of San Francisco. Within a few minutes, dozens of students had signed in and settled into their seats to finish breakfast. When breakfast was over, Cathrine Sneed stood in front and called for a meditation period over the talking and laughing of the students. It took only a minute for the stillness of meditation to overtake the room.

Ten minutes later, Sneed began the class: "Demetrius counts sixty-one students, sixty-one *special* students, sixty-one miracles. You encourage me to find funding for you. I want you to be encouraged like I am as I look out on this group today." She reminded them to apply for courses at City College, explaining that the dean wants to help them get back into school and has opened the school for them to use.

"Tomorrow there will be a press conference at the garden. On the surface it's to announce a study of the Horticulture Project; the real agenda is the new three strikes law. How many of you have two prior felonies?" Dozens of hands hit the air. "How many have three?" Hands went up slowly, reluctantly—first a few, then many.

The day's lesson was the plight of one of their own. Sneed told about Mark Coates, who had called her the previous night from jail: "Mark was in the Horticulture Project at San Bruno, but I threw him out because he wouldn't get serious. He came to the Garden Project three years later serious about himself. When he was stopped by the police yesterday, he was driving with a suspended license. He was driving with a suspended license and 'mistakenly' gave the police his brother's name. (They laugh.) Mark was charged with resisting arrest and he already has two felonies. (They groan.) Mark stands to lose his auto mechanics class and his *high- paying* job at the Garden Project. (They laugh.) But I can't spend my day rescuing sixty-one of you. What I'd like you to think about today is this. Some of you have warrants. We can help arrange for you to do community service. Mark has a little baby, and I know that when he's driving around, he's driving with that little baby. Look inside yourself. Warrants . . . tickets . . . I could go to a judge and work out a community service project. Parking tickets can be taken care of with community service."

"We get stopped just 'cause we look like criminals," a student called out.

"Rolling probable cause," Sneed quipped. She told about being pulled over once on her way to work by a white police officer, after she took an illegal left turn. "Pull the fuck over," he yelled, kicking her door. He gave Sneed a ticket even after she showed him her sheriff's department ID.

"If we have a warrant from out of town, can we do community service here?" one student asked.

Sneed continued, "I'll ask Sheriff Michael Hennessey what can be done. *But I am asking all of you to do what we can to be a free people.*"

Cathrine announced that they would be cleaning streets and weeding around tree-pits at an elementary school for the rest of the morning. Their community service has already begun—in the clearing and cleaning of parks, playgrounds, schools, and senior centers that she has organized with this "work crew." But more than community service is going on. As Sneed frequently points out, "I would like to see my students working with seniors—the people they have stolen purses from. If they clean the grounds of a senior housing project and plant a garden with the seniors, they could never steal their purses again."

The class of sixty-one men and women, plus some young children brought by a few parents, headed for the morning's assignment in high spirits. Walking past a corner where a few young men were selling crack, one student chided a crack dealer to join them instead. Without waiting for instruction, the group split up into work crews. Some with plastic bags began picking up litter and pulling weeds in tree-pits, on sidewalks, and on the curb; they were followed by others with brooms, rakes, and shovels. No one appeared to be giving orders or overseeing the job, but the discipline and focus of the students put any public works department to shame. Some students wanted to scale the chain link fence and continue the spring cleanup in the elementary school playground until they were deterred by Cathrine Sneed, who reminded them that they were encroaching on the school janitor's turf. An hour later the work crew, high on the good feeling of a job well done, posed for a picture in front of their most recent community service.

Cathrine Sneed introduced Jaquan Dontez Rice as one of the Garden Project "stars." At eighteen he already seemed old. Jaquan described himself as a "teenage parent" who had his first child at fourteen. Now he was "trying to start on life" and take his "first step into the real world." Otherwise, "there's just straight negatives." Focusing on the positive place where he's going in life, he said that the field he would like to study is "communicating." When he talks, he likes to try to send electricity. "Ever since I was little, I was able to communicate—any race, any age, handicapped, unhandicapped." He was student body president in eighth grade, but he got involved in drug dealing and gang warfare and never finished school. He was saved, he says, by being caught as a juvenile, held a day, and put on probation. Reality, because he looked it in the face and communicated with it, saved him too: He has two kids. Now he's attending the Southeast Campus of City College three evenings a week, encouraged in the Garden Project to get his GED and then a college degree, maybe in social work:

As I got older and saw my daughter growing, I thought 'You make less, but you make more in the long run.' This is the first job I ever had in my life, the first commitment I ever made. I would never give up on this. This is for my kids. I gave up 'cause of no high school education. This was like a blessing for me. Everyday I'm better in myself, the less I feel like being around negatives. I live in Alice Griffith Project. All drug stuff is happening there right outside the front door where my kids would play. I don't have a bank account. I talk to the Man Upstairs.

Jaquan Dontez Rice.

A woman who had just finished raking a freshly weeded corner introduced Cathrine Sneed to her cousin, saying he wanted to join the project. Cathrine handed him a packet with job information, a contract, and w-4 forms, and told him to join them tomorrow morning.

An accountant might have advised Cathrine Sneed to turn the woman's cousin away. Finances are tight; the project would survive more easily if she kept it to twenty students. But this is more than a business, and the students' work is more than a job. "It's why they come; because they could make a lot more than $5.50 an hour on the street." And it's why they return even when the program periodically runs out of money. Yet if the Garden Project were funded with even one-quarter the money it saves federal taxpayers by keeping these sixty-one students out of the criminal justice turnstile—approximately $30,000 per student per year in operating costs and $50,000 per new cell construction—its books would balance.

Alice Waters, chef and owner of the restaurant Chez Panisse, encouraged President Clinton, when he was dining at her restaurant, to visit the garden that grew the signature radishes she serves. Not only could he learn to improve his diet, not only would he encounter a low-cost model of crime prevention based on fundamentals of beauty, honesty, and integrity, he would also find food restored to its place in culture as a nourishing gift. The philosopher-chef praises the Garden Project for incorporating everything that she thinks is important about food: "digging in the ground, planting, husbanding, harvesting, cooking, preserving, putting it out on the table, serving it to your friends and family, and sharing it with them." The President hasn't made it to the garden yet.

Many students have said that Cathrine Sneed changed their lives. As she sees it, she taught them how to garden, the garden gave them something good—a feeling of faith in themselves—that they had never had, and then *they changed* their lives. "I have seen this program make people have hope who had no hope, when they grow food at San Bruno for people who have no food, when they plant and tend trees on city streets in the Mission district that have no trees, when they grow flowers at Hunter's Point where there were no flowers." It is not herself and not her staff, Sneed insists, "it's working with those green things" that gives these women and men a sense of life that most have never felt anywhere else.

Why the garden as school? The garden, Sneed explains, is an excellent classroom for students who never did well in school, who failed there and were punished and maybe expelled. There, they lost the only chance they might have had to become literate and competent in society; their hopes ended with failure in school. Her students are resources that have been labeled waste, and, like a master gardener of life, she set out to reclaim them. The garden is an affordable school for the "strong poor" who don't have fees for college.

The "strong poor"—for example, the farmers dispossessed of land in John Steinbeck's *The Grapes of Wrath*—reminded Cathrine Sneed of the inmates she counseled at San Bruno, and were the spark that started the Garden Project. In the early 1980s, Sneed was in the hospital, gravely ill with a rare kidney disease, when a friend gave her a copy of *The Grapes of Wrath*. The characters,

ABOVE:
*Gardeners
selecting radishes
and cabbage
leaves for* Chez
Panisse.

RIGHT:
*Vegetables
packaged for the
restaurant.*

the story, and the land, combined with Sneed's heightened sense of her own mortality, helped to clarify things. She asked Sheriff Hennessey to let her start an organic garden project at the county jail if she recovered. Hennessey respected her work, and recalled that the county jail in San Bruno was built on 145 acres of land that had been farmed in the 1930s. Furthermore, Sneed's prognosis wasn't good. How could he turn down a friend and colleague who was dying? As for Cathrine, she wondered if anyone in America in the 1980s would respect working with the soil. Hadn't farming lost its dignity to a briefcase? But the independence and strength of the prostituted women she had worked with in smoke-filled cells at San Bruno reminded her of the "strong poor" she read about in *The Grapes of Wrath*. That clinched her decision.

The Beginnings

In 1982 a recovered Cathrine Sneed brought four inmates out to the garden site—against the instincts of some jail administrators, who predicted that the new prison population "would hurt her" and "would run." One of her first students was a man named Forrest who had a three-decade-long criminal history that included ten arrests for assault with a deadly weapon. The inmates, working without tools or gloves, tore down old buildings and cleaned a brush- and bramble-tangled site. With a budget of three hundred dollars scraped together by the sheriff and friends, Cathrine bought seeds and garden supplies for her first class of ten students. Forrest "busted his butt and became a kick-ass radish grower," she says, and seeing the garden transform him gave her hope that she could "do something about this world."

Had she not been dying, Sneed says that she wouldn't have been moved to start the garden. But, "as I was able to recover, it's the same with them." Since 1982, thousands of men and women have worked on the eight-acre farm, and have harvested tens of thousands of crates worth of potatoes, corn, spinach, beets, Russian kale, mustard greens, beans, herbs, and flowers. The food they have grown has fed thousands of the homeless people of San Francisco in soup kitchens such as Martin de Poores and the Episcopal Sanctuary, and also through Project Openhand, which brings food to homebound AIDS patients.

One man explained the new feelings of love and the lesson of respect for other humans that he has learned from working in the greenhouse at San Bruno. Every day he watered plants, transplanted seedlings, and cleaned the greenhouse. "What I am doing is *feeding myself* with love for plants. I never knew I had these feelings inside of me, now I do." He applied the simple lesson of a plant living if you "treat it right" and dying if you "treat it wrong" to people in the jail: "I'm a Latino from my heart. I don't feel less than nobody. Even I don't feel more than nobody . . . But many people confuse that . . . Being here, working in the greenhouse is gonna help people. You gotta work with people you never seen before and don't know how they think."

Another student found out what a garden has to do with his life when he

Carroll Street Garden Participation Contract

I agree to participate in the Garden Project's Carroll Street Garden Program, a community service and job skills training program designed to help me take responsibility for my life. I have voluntarily joined the program, and understand that I am free to leave at any time.

As a participant, I will be assigned to a schedule of work, classes, and other activities through which I can become a better worker and a more responsible individual.

I, (Please print your name)_____ agree to abide by all the rules of the Carroll Street Garden Program:

I will treat myself and others with dignity and respect.
I will be on time to work and for all Garden Project commitments.
I agree to focus on myself and my work at all times.
I will stay drug and alcohol free at all times.
I will be honest and truthful with my peers and supervisors.
I will accept the direction of all Garden Project staff.
If I break this agreement I will be dismissed immediately.

Signed (Garden Project Student): _____Date _____
Signed (Garden Project Supervisor): _____Date_____

Job Description: Garden Project Student

Garden Project Students are responsible for working under the direction of Garden Project Staff to plant, harvest, and maintain the Carroll Street Garden. Work includes preparing beds for planting, moving and sifting compost, planting seedlings, weeding, watering, and harvesting organic produce. As participants in the Garden Project's Carroll Street Program, Garden Project Students will be required to participate in a variety of activities outside their work that are designed to improve themselves. Some of these activities may include seeing a counselor, attending classes at City College of San Francisco, and attending Alcoholics Anonymous or Narcotic Anonymous meetings.

planted a bean. For that bean to grow, he had to plant it a certain depth, apply some lime, and keep it watered and weeded. "Hey, if I can take care of this fava bean, why can't I take care of myself?" Without hesitation a woman student said, "Flowers are my thing. I take care of my beautiful yard behind me," as she pointed to the beds of flowers she tends in the jail garden. "I come out here and talk to my flowers, tell them I love them, water them. When I see the dead ones, I pick them off so the others have a chance to grow."

Everyone in jail knows first-hand the soup kitchens their vegetables and herbs supply: Often these students have been among the hungry and homeless in line. "It gives you motivation," said a student named Heather. "Every time we're picking something and putting it in a crate, we know where it's going and that it's gonna help somebody." Another added a point about restitution: "We took a lot out of our community and this is a way of giving back to our community by growing produce for them. We grow the best and give the best to the people."

But what happens to people like Forrest, and the woman whose flower garden in jail became her very own beautiful yard, when their time in jail and in the Horticulture Project is up? The problem is that "when they [leave] jail, they [are] leaving the best thing that happened in their life." Danny, one of Cathrine's students at San Bruno, described himself as a "dead tree" when he first came to the garden in jail; but he saw that, like a tree which grows and bears fruit when it is watered and fed, he thrived as he worked in the garden. He talked passionately about his pumpkin patch—not believing when he planted the seeds that they would grow, then astonished as they grew, and finally proud to give his pumpkins away to visitors at the jail. Danny wanted to work on a farm when he left jail; he wanted to be "dedicated to the farm" like he was to the garden. "I wanna work just as hard and I wanna stay clean." He spoke for all of the horticulture students at San Bruno when he pleaded for some place to go from jail: "We need jobs, we need money to keep this thing going. We need a shelter when we leave here . . . a place to go when they drop you at 850 Bryant St. What are you gonna do—walk up 6th Street to the liquor store? We gotta start a horticulture project on the outside to keep this thing going."

But Danny, who pleaded to go from jail to a farm, walked back up 6th Street to the liquor store and died on the streets from having his head bashed in. What upset Cathrine Sneed most was not even that her students went back to the street when they left jail—most had no other place to go—but that they were

Harvesting at the Hunter's Point garden.

happy to return to jail so they could work in the garden. So, in 1991 she launched the Garden Project on a half-acre in Hunter's Point/Bayview, San Francisco, for horticulture students leaving San Bruno: part market garden with a business plan; part community service, with students doing cleanups and greenups in the neighborhoods they have hurt; and part visionary model for eradicating the social injustices that spawn criminality.

California Crops

When Elliot Hoffmann showed it to Cathrine Sneed, the half-acre at Hunter's Point was derelict and dumped-on land, sandwiched between commerce and industry. She had approached the successful founder of Just Desserts for a donation to buy tools for her project; he talked about establishing a market garden for post-release inmates on land behind his commercial bakery. He suggested growing strawberries that he could buy, and proposed the idea of training and hiring some of her gardeners in his bakery. Like thousands of gardens in Harlem, Chicago, and North Philadelphia, the Garden Project commenced with a major cleanup, and became an oasis of beauty, tranquillity, and nature amid noise, pollution, traffic, and poverty.

Most of the county jail inmates reside in seven low-income neighborhoods of San Francisco. Hunter's Point/Bayview, primarily an African-American community, is one of them. (San Francisco's only designated Superfund site, the naval shipyard, is also in Hunter's Point). What better place to site the Garden Project than in the neighborhood in which many students live—as a local, tangible symbol of the changes they are making in their lives? The second geographical asset was its proximity to the Just Desserts commercial bakery, a partner in developing the garden. The bakery purchases produce from the garden, provides day-old baked goods that are set out on a picnic table in the garden, and makes bathroom facilities available to students. Side-by-side, the garden and the bakery symbolize Cathrine Sneed's long-term vision of partnerships between income-generating gardens, orchards, and tree nurseries, and local businesses, restaurants, and markets.

Students divide their weekly twenty-hour work week between community service projects at schools and community centers throughout Hunter's Point, and working in the market garden. In raised beds that they have carefully built from compost and manure, they cultivate Russian and American kale, mustard greens, arugula, garlic, radishes, chives, peas, celery, carrots, spinach, Chinese

Children smelling flowers at Hunter's Point.

A CLASS OF STARS

cabbage, and herbs. They harvest young greens and baby vegetables, then sort, select, and pack the best for restaurants that buy their produce. On one typical day the harvest includes four cartons of radishes, arugula, chives, and Chinese cabbage, laid between layers of wetted newspaper to keep them fresh for Chez Panisse in Berkeley. Strawberries are sold to Just Desserts, and eventually maybe flowers to the San Francisco flower market. Flowers are everywhere in the garden—California poppies, carnations, alyssum, ajuga, daisies, forget-me-nots, and daffodils. "Food on the table is not enough," says Cathrine Sneed, who encourages students to take home flowers. "Flowers are as important as vegetables" in this pedagogy of plants that feed the body and also the soul.

"We're thinking about calling our produce 'California Crops,'" said Shawn Smith, who has emerged as a garden philosopher-in-residence and mentor to others in the project. This garden project, he observed, is not for everybody. "People who get into this project have to *care about life*." If they care about life, "their seeds will sprout." The garden isn't for impatient people—"you can't rush nature, you can't rush life." About life's good moments Shawn says, "you memorize them and make them reoccur." As for the bad moments, "you learn from them and turn them around." Tory, another gardener, talked about how working in the garden and talking with Shawn eased his stress. "You can be weeding a bed, and it's like weeding your life." He can come out to the garden and dig a trench for a deep bed by himself and be alone, or do it with Shawn and talk about his hard times with his woman friend. "Life," Shawn said, "you gotta let it bloom. Every day I feel like I started something." Both young men moved on to political topics as they weeded a celery patch. About equal opportunity in the workplace: "Guys shouldn't complain; there are plenty of smart women out there." About foreign aid: "Why not invest in U.S. cities. We have a war here with gangs." About the human dimension of the garden: "Each person has something to offer. This man—he can sing. Maybe he can teach the others to sing." Nearby, Angela Williams spoke up as she worked a patch of Russian kale with a woman friend: "I give my all and all from the heart. It keeps a smile on your face."

Facing Page and Left: *Hunter's Point gardeners.*

There's a lot of love in this market garden and school of life, love which counteracts the lovelessness of a society that incarcerates better than it educates and leaves one-fifth of its children hungry and poor. There are also a lot of stars here. Cathrine Sneed will introduce one student as "a star," and later, another as "a star," until, with enough introductions and enough time, every student has been called "a star" for one attribute or another. The Garden Project, tended by students whose spark first dimmed and disappeared in the public schools, is a class of stars.

The Tree Corps

I heard the president talk about planting a million trees.
—Student, San Bruno horticulture class

A billion trees. But you know what? If we don't do it, the planet isn't going to be here. But it's not just trees, they've got to start planting you guys. Let's start a tree corps and pay you to make a new life and save the planet. I like that . . . a tree corps. (Students applaud.)
—Cathrine Sneed

Ten of the Garden Project stars now form an elite crew called the Tree Corps, a nonprofit organization which Cathrine Sneed and the sheriff's department were instrumental in creating in 1992. They have secured a contract with the city of San Francisco for the Tree Corps to plant and maintain trees in Hunter's Point, the Mission, and other low-income areas of the city—neighborhoods where the person planting the tree may have an uncle or brother or granddaughter. Maria Centano is one of two women on the crew. "I do every part of this work and love every piece of it. I started at the jail garden but I never expected it would change my life. What I like best is that when I plant a tree, I leave something here, beyond me, after me. I try to identify the tree by its botanical name when I drive by with my grandchildren and children." She explained that the tree crew has to learn to spell the Latin names of trees, and to identify trees by their bark and leaves. When they are on break in the nursery, they walk around and test themselves. She gave an example: *Melaleuca quinquenervia.*

With two other students, Rumaldo and Ephrem, Maria has been in the Tree Corps from its beginning. She described how "the garden and Cathy" changed her life. "For years I used and sold drugs on the street; always in pain and always looking over my shoulder, I thought I would die on the streets." In jail she joined the Horticulture Project, but the Garden Project didn't exist when she left jail the first time. "I fell back into the streets. I felt I was selling drugs by force, that I had no choice because I didn't feel I could do anything else." The second time she left jail, Maria joined the newly started Garden Project in Hunter's Point; and, as Cathrine Sneed would put it, "the green things" gave her a sense of the possible, and she changed her life.

Maria and the whole crew work forty hours a week at eight dollars an hour. With her paycheck she is paying the Catholic school tuition for her grandchild—$180 per month—doing for her what she didn't do for her own children. "Being incarcerated doesn't help anyone. When they come out they're scared and come back to the same thing. We need more programs like this." Knowing first-hand the struggle for redemption, she gives advice to people still using drugs, and thinks of working as a drug counselor when she is too old to plant trees. No longer, she said with the soulful relief of one freed from a great existential burden, does she have to look over her shoulder. "Right now I'm high on life."

The Tree Corps crew worked in pairs putting in new trees on Valencia Street between 15th and 16th Streets in late March 1994. In forty-five minutes, Tom Wong and Maurice Branch have planted a young *Tristania conferta*. The Brisbane box, as it is commonly known, is a subtropical evergreen tree, excellent for city sidewalks, supervisor Jerous Sneed (Cathrine's brother) explained, "because it grows up more than out and is a size that won't damage the sidewalk." The crew will maintain the new trees they have planted by watering, weeding, and mulching them regularly. Tom Wong described his teamwork with Maurice Branch as "a fast and fluid chain reaction" and rattled off the steps of planting a tree that they have just completed:

Dig a two-foot by two-foot hole.
Drop in a plastic root restricter.
Install and center the tree.
Fill in and pack soil around the tree, making sure the root crown is
   above the root restricter.
Berm around the tree for good water catchment.
Pound in protective posts on both sides of the tree to a depth of
   2½ feet; put in a crosspiece to stabilize the sticks.
Straighten the tree and tie straps from the tree to the posts to hold
   and protect the tree from rubbing against the crosspiece.
Water with about 5 gallons.
Secure the protective wire cage to the posts.

Tom Wong dropped out of high school because he couldn't stand the confinement of a classroom or office. He likes working with his hands, and he prefers working with trees to auto mechanics "'cause cars are killing us. When you plant something, you're planting a new self. When I come back in a few weeks and see this healthy tree, I'll think this is for my children and grandchildren." He confided that while he doesn't have any children of his own, he does have a godchild, and his co-worker Maurice has children, so the tree he planted "can be for them." Although Tom was never in jail, he was forced as a teenager to join a gang, and was homeless for a time. Cathrine Sneed accepted him into

66

The Tree Corps.

the Garden Project and he "worked hard so she would recommend me to the Tree Corps. Eight dollars an hour doesn't put a lot of money in my pocket, but my heart and head feel great." As Tom talked, Rumaldo, a senior on the crew, and the supervisor Jerous examined the tree that Tom and Maurice planted. They showed the young men how to adjust the support straps to better protect the tree from being grazed by the crosspiece.

Cathrine Sneed often read Jean Giono's *The Man Who Planted Trees* to horticulture students in jail. It is the story of a desolate, desiccated part of Provence that had lost trees, wildlife, and streams, and was abandoned by people, except for a solitary shepherd. The shepherd gathered acorns, selected the best, and planted them—one hundred thousand in three years, and then many thousands more, oak and beech and birch, over the span of two world wars—because the "land was dying for want of trees." In time the young trees grew into forest and wild animals returned; rain soaked into the forest soil and replenished groundwater; once-dry brooks coursed with water, and wetland and flood-plain vegetation reappeared; the dry, searing wind was buffered and moistened, and people came to restore villages and verdant farms.

What could be more dissimilar than the "barren and colorless" land of Provence, denuded for charcoal-making, where nothing grew but wild lavender and no one lived but one silent shepherd—and the noisy, congested, gritty Mission district and Hunter's Point, or a county jail? Yet both the shepherd who planted trees in Provence and the inmates and ex-inmates who plant gardens and trees in the city are leaving their marks upon the earth, "sprung from the hands and the soul . . . without technical resources." A chain reaction is also taking place in Hunter's Point and the Mission as flowers, vegetables, and trees are planted on derelict lots and greenless streets. For one garden inspires another garden; one street cleanup and greenup encourages another; grandchildren learn the Latin names of trees from their grandmother, who planted them; local businesses buy from and hire from their community; and people who had no exit are given an entry. This modern-day morality tale about the saving grace of a singular human, and the ecological literacy that the garden projects teach, share a common ethic: Nature often awaits the restorative touch of humans, and conversely, nature often restores love and hope where humans have failed. After hearing the story, an inmate later wrote to tell Cathrine that the story "inspired me to learn to read because it was so beautiful that I wanted to be able to read it myself."

The Garden Project 2000

Rolled up in the corner of the Garden Project's office is a mural of ideas and images, titled The Garden Project 2000, that captures just how far the Garden Project could go. It is the outcome of a meeting coordinated by BBC Associates, a consulting company that donated office space to the Garden Project and is committed to working with them on strategic planning. BBC doesn't believe in starting with a problem and strategizing how to solve it; rather, they start with dreams and ideals and brainstorm how to achieve them. In September 1991 they proposed a session of "visioning" with Cathrine Sneed, Sheriff Michael Hennessey, Angela Davis, and a group of practical visionaries, including people from foundations and progressive businesses, such as Just Desserts and Ben and Jerry's. "For the first time," said Sneed about the process and outcome, "I knew I wasn't crazy. I talked about what I wanted and the group understood and we took it from there."

Unfurled, the mural spans some twenty feet of wall, depicting themes of community service both in jail and beyond that mingle with the ideals of green teams in cities and green political parties. A transformation that begins with gardens, art, and literacy in jail leads to ex-prisoners becoming teachers, artists, and lawyers who not only continue to do community gardening, but who work to eradicate the adverse life circumstances that spawn crime.

FACING PAGE: *Sharing lunch at Hunter's Point.*

These grand dreams require a financial plan and the institutional capacity to follow through. Unless jobs are created and small businesses start up, unless funding is assured, Cathrine Sneed tells every audience, the ambitious agenda will be foreshortened and forestalled. Her business plan for the next three to five years includes expanding the tree planting and maintenance contract with San Francisco's Department of Public Works, and launching new market gardens to supply produce for Bay Area restaurants. Start-up capital has been raised from foundations, and a membership drive is being launched. One of her long-term goals is to garner government investment as an alternative to capital outlays for prison building—one reason why Alice Waters is determined to get President Clinton to visit the Garden Project.

Contrasting natural resource protection with this model of urban environmentalism, Cathrine Sneed said: "You can buy up land to protect it, all it takes is money. You can't buy people to protect them, it takes love and years of work." The Garden Project is far more than a horticultural version of New Age spirituality, as one journalist described it, or an alternative twelve-step program to get people clean and sober. Cathrine Sneed, who ran away as a teenager to join a revolution at the zenith of the Civil Rights and Black Power movements, is now engaged in creating one. In the process of giving back to the community they have harmed—through planting gardens in schools where they may have failed, in day care centers where their children play, and in senior centers where someone whom they have robbed may live—her students engage in what Paulo Freire calls "the incessant struggle to gain their humanity." In challenging the model of "manhood" that uses language degrading to women, that walks away from children, and that gets its power from drugs and alcohol; in talking of strength as caring for one's children the way one does for one's seedlings; in planting their students into the saving environment of gardens while teaching them the skills of planting and the love of trees, Cathrine Sneed and Arlene Hamilton turn a closed, no-exit world into a limited one that their students have a chance to transform.

Fannie Lou Hamer learned at age forty-four that she had the right to vote, and the plantation worker went on to demand an end to all-white delegations at the 1964 Democratic National Convention. Perhaps a student of this new freedom school — Maria Centano, the grandmother who plants trees, or Jaquan Dontez Rice, who likes to send electricity when he speaks — will arise, as Fannie Lou Hamer did from the Mississippi Freedom School, and shake the conscience of a country that incarcerates more decisively than it educates.

PHILADELPHIA:
A City of Neighborhoods

PREVIOUS PAGE:
*A young
gardener from
Project Rainbow.*
(Photo by Mary
Van Muelken)

Philadelphia city gardeners share their vision of the possible garden in the impossible environment of alienated city blocks . . . The seed on the wind does not discriminate where it falls. It finds a home even in the crack of the concrete. This is what the city gardener knows.

—Bilge Friedlaender

"I AM AN ELECTED OFFICIAL, BUT *THESE TWO WOMEN ARE LEADERS*," Councilman Dan McElhatton proclaimed. "To those who say that whites and Latinos cannot get along, come to Norris Square. To those who say the cities are not worth saving, come to Norris Square, see it." We stood in *Las Parcelas* on September 17, 1993, oblivious of the saturnine sky and the oncoming rain, and applauded as Tomasita Romero and Iris Brown received gold-plated shovels from Philadelphia Green's Executive Director J. Blaine Bonham. The event— the dedication festival of Philadelphia Green's eighth (and first Hispanic) Greene Countrie Towne—was called *Escándalo* by the community, loosely meaning "a wonderful event that people would talk about for a very long time."

The demonstration compost project and environmental park, the eleven tree-lined blocks, and the fifty-nine flower and vegetable gardens which comprise the Norris Square Greene Countrie Towne are a "dream for everybody," Iris Brown told us. *Las Parcelas* is its centerpiece, with sixteen family vegetable plots; an orchard planted with peaches, pears, nectarines, and grapes; *La Casita* (a small traditional Puerto Rican house built by neighbors); perennial and herb gardens; ornamental grasses; and a patio for cookouts. Iris credited a group of ten women ("they are," she added, "humble and speak no English") who have done most of the work. The women call themselves *motivos*—ones who are motivated and who want to motivate others. During the winter they meet weekly to discuss Puerto Rican history, see films, and enjoy Latino food and music; during the growing season they cultivate the many Norris Square neighborhood gardens.

"I have seen things good, not so good, the pits—this is the best time of the past thirty years." Tomasita Romero recounted the upturn after the three troubled decades during which she has lived in Norris Square:

This neighborhood was one of the worst areas in drugs, known as the *Badlands*. The community came together—Anglos, Dominicans,

Cubans, Puerto Ricans, blacks—and formed United Neighbors Against Drugs. Twenty to forty of us met at Norris Square Park and walked the neighborhood every evening, lingering on corners where the largest drug dealing went on.

She cited Sister Carol Keck, executive director of the Norris Square Neighborhood Project, who pioneered environmental education for children in the community-run environmental learning center. It was Sister Keck who wrote to Philadelphia Green, the citywide greening organization sponsored by the Pennsylvania Horticulture Society, requesting that they commit resources to the Hispanic neighborhood. Philadelphia Green "believed in us," she continued, "believed that we could work together." For four years, from 1989 to 1993, the greening organization worked with the Norris Square community gardeners, teachers, children, *motivos*, and neighborhood leaders, to design and implement a master plan that would help rescue the twenty-block neighborhood of three thousand people with a lifeline made of gardens, trees, and horticulturally beautiful, culturally rich open spaces.

"This community had nowhere to go but up," commented Don Haskin, a vice president of Provident National Bank, who attended the *Escándalo*. "The ninety-six greening projects in Norris Square are a testament to how people want to create great neighborhoods and stability." He cited the links between community organizations like the Norris Square Civic Association, whose focus is rehabilitating housing and building new housing with community-based builders, and the Norris Square Greening Committee, whose president is Tomasita Romero. These partnerships, and the sense of neighborhood and community that is felt in gardens such as *Las Parcelas* and nearby *Raices* ("roots") and *El Batey* ("place of retreat"), have put Norris Square on an upswing that has attracted the bank's investment. "Banks go block-by-block in evaluating credit-worthiness for mortgages," said Haskin. "It is much more likely homeowners will qualify for mortgages on a block improved by Philadelphia Green." Since 1992, Provident National Bank has also donated $250,000 as a sponsor of the annual Philadelphia Flower Show, the profits of which fund a significant portion of Philadelphia Green's annual budget.

The historical life cycle of Norris Square is a woeful one repeated in dozens, if not hundreds, of northeastern cities and mill towns dominated and then deserted by industrialists. Once heavily forested land of the Leni-Lenape Indian territory, Norris Square was given to Quaker Isaac Norris in 1693 by William Penn. Penn's vision for the city he founded was that of a "greene countrie towne" where "care would be taken to leave one acre of trees for every five acres cleared." He was—after the Incas and Aztecs—one of the first town planners of the Americas to design public gardens into urban projects.

By the late eighteenth century, Philadelphia was a thriving, entrepreneurial town of artisans and shopkeepers, most working out of the front rooms of houses which sprang up in a jumble, unheeding of Penn's orderly exhortation. Kitchen and market gardens, with herbs, vegetables, flowers, and fruit trees, survived in backyards and on patches of open space and neighborhood peripheries. By the second half of the nineteenth century, the city had industrialized faster and more fully than any other American city. Factories producing machines and metal parts, lamps and gas fixtures, furniture, clothing, hats, and carpets, concentrated in a handful of neighborhoods. Industrialists transmogrified cities from diverse settlements of shops, cottages, and gardens into monotonic brick, mortar, and asphalt.

Norris Square became one of those sooty mill town neighborhoods. Every patch of verdant land was cleared and crammed with attached houses for workers and mammoth factories, laid out in a grid pattern. Thousands of English, Scottish, Irish, and German immigrant weavers arrived to work in its lace, hosiery, carpet, and textile factories. Not a tidbit of nature was spared in the dense factory neighborhood for dooryard gardens. A tiny backyard held the privy and coal bin; but gardens that had served to compost human and animal waste, to provide fresh food, and to drain rain and wastewater from habitats, were sacrificed to land-intensive industrialization. Only a solitary park, Norris Square Park, remained as a remnant of the once heavily forested land and memory of the maxim to spare one acre of trees for every five cleared.

Today, in this largely Hispanic neighborhood where German, Irish, Korean, Polish, African-American, Vietnamese, and Palestinian people also live, empty factories and vacant housing lots littered with shards of brick and concrete testify to its desperate economic decomposition in the latter half of the twentieth century. The causes for the decline of Norris Square and the surrounding neighborhoods of North Philadelphia are the same forces that have nearly extinguished the life of many eastern and rust belt cities over the past forty years: the exodus of the white middle, lower middle, and working classes from the crowded center of the city to suburbs at its periphery; corporate relocation away from inner cities to suburban office parks and developing countries; "redlining" by financial institutions, the practice of not investing in certain inner-city neighborhoods so that few residents, regardless of their creditworthiness, got mortgages, insurance, and business loans; federal cutbacks in aid to cities; and the drain of money from cities by the military budget. Between 1960 and 1987, per capita income in cities dropped from 105 percent of the per capita income in surrounding suburbs to 57 percent. Thus cities face a fiscal crisis from the shrinking tax base. An October 1991 report by the Federal Reserve found that Latinos and African-Americans were refused home mortgages more than twice as often as whites of the same level of income. Between 1980 and 1992, the federal share of city budgets dropped from 14.3 percent to less than 5 percent. In 1990 taxpayers in nineteen of the twenty-five largest cities paid more money in taxes to the defense budget than flowed back into those cities as industry contracts and jobs.

How, then, does a garden planted by local children and women begin to redress the quotidian blight of an inner-city neighborhood? Or are *Raices*, with its native plants and mural of Puerto Rico's cultural roots, and *El Batey*, with its ancient Taino Indian ceremonial symbols of spirals, suns, and animal faces

Iris Brown in El Batey garden.

Facing Page: *Taino Indian ceremonial stones in the El Batey garden.*

painted on flagstones, only a respite from an implacable reality? A palliative where a cure is needed? What, if any, is the capacity of these heritage gardens to restore city life?

Urban analysts point to three initiatives that are necessary to revitalize the economy and rebuild cities: investing in the nation's infrastructure, including roads, bridges, and public transportation; expanding social programs such as education, job training, health and child care, to enable people to work; and "knitting together the fabric of urban neighborhoods." Iris Brown is a teacher in the Norris Square Neighborhood Project and she understands—through the impress of inner-city life—the links between education, job training, and employment opportunities. She knows what community greening can and cannot do for children.

> I cannot promise them they're going to get a good education. I
> cannot promise them they are going to graduate from high school or
> go to college. I cannot tell them they will have a job. I can tell them
> they will have fresh produce to eat; I can promise them they will have
> beauty.

She can also promise children that they will grow up in a neighborhood unified by its successful struggle to evict major drug dealers and drug trafficking, a neighborhood where the cultural and botanical legacy of Puerto Ricans fills vacant lots that once had been taken as if by eminent domain by drug dealers. She can promise them what no amount of income and no amount of security systems, guards, guns, and locks in suburbs and new towns can buy—the hard-woven fabric of neighborhood. She can promise that the gardens, with their murals, sculpture, and horticulture, will exhibit the artistry of the informally-trained artists of their community. And if the gardens offer, as Alice Walker wrote of her mother's flower garden, the space and time apart from shabbiness and menial, low-wage work for the artist to arise, then perhaps the writers, the sculptors, and the composers of Norris Square will arise in children as they celebrate their birthdays in *Raices* and plant with the *motivos* in *El Batey*.

Iris Brown recalled having to hire a private security guard when she first held environmental education classes in Norris Square Park. "I can't measure what the gardens do. Drugs don't just destroy a person, they destroy families and neighborhoods. If we suggested cleaning up a neighborhood, people just laughed. When the shooting started, there were smaller and smaller places to hide." Not even her home was a refuge—she can trace the path of a bullet that entered her mother's house and lodged in a living-room wall. She told how members of United Neighbors Against Drugs stood all night on corners where the most drug dealing went on, and stopped it. Then, in the first year of greening that followed, when people saw that the gardens weren't being vandalized, "they got motivated." Of the core group of women whom she credits for the Greene Countrie Towne Brown said, "it is better to have a group of ten or twelve *motivos* than to have a whole community not motivated." She repeated a joke circulating about the gardens to illustrate the upwelling community pride in Norris Square: "If we charged for every person who goes by the gardens, we would be rich. We could rent *La Casita* and make lots of money."

Future gardens will have Puerto Rican vegetables such as *gandules*, or pigeon peas, which are high in iron; coriander; and yautia. "People see them and get *nostálgico*. I mean, the plants take you back to what you are, something you can't get from a place that's not fundamentally your own." Iris talked of "planting more herbs than ever," explaining that in Puerto Rico she grew up taking herbs when she was sick. She recognizes some of the weeds on former housing lots in the neighborhood as plants that were collected for remedies and cooking in Puerto Rico. When she invites women to speak to the *motivos* about herbal remedies, "no one wants to go home." The gardens with their art, sculpture, rites, and botanical history embody the culture of her heart—so evident at the Norris Square Greene Countrie Towne dedication festival as she, luminous under a leaden sky, explained the Taino Indian symbols and pointed to the root crop which Puerto Ricans used to make bread, growing in the *El Batey* garden.

The gardens have reinvigorated for Iris Brown the value of the traditional, evanescent culture of medicinal herbs she left, a culture she intends to transmit to Latinos and Anglos alike. She has bought a small house in Puerto Rico and talks of returning there for an extended period to study with Faustino, a seventy-seven-year-old herbalist renowned for his knowledge of plants and their remedies. "It's like the rain forest . . . when he goes, everything goes with him. The old people and Indians have the knowledge but it will disappear with them."

Philadelphia Green, which worked four years with this community, enjoys its own *nostálgico* in this Hispanic Greene Countrie Towne, for every block greened with trees and gardens conjures up Penn's plan of "an acre of trees for every five acres cleared." A full one-third of the 2200 block of North Palethorp Street is taken up by the garden and orchard called *Las Parcelas*. Behind it is *Parque Pasivo Eslabones*, a park named for the links, or *eslabones*, between families and the community, between generations, and between the neighborhood and Puerto Rico. This former asphalt-covered vacant lot is planted with native Pennsylvania trees and shrubs, species that had established themselves in the forests of the Leni-Lenape.

The map of Norris Square Greene Countrie Towne reveals a startling likeness to the original plan for the new Quaker town, amid the extraordinary changes of private wealth-building, industrialism, and the elimination of nature over the course of three hundred years in this oldest of American industrial cities. The first engraved version of Penn's plan for Philadelphia shows a rectangle of land stretching from the Delaware River to the Schuylkill, divided into individual plots that allowed for gardens, orchards, and fields. Drawn in 1683—ten years before Penn granted nearby land to Isaac Norris—the engraving depicts a central park square, where City Hall stands today, and four residential park squares equidistant from the center. Of the four, only Rittenhouse Square has remained a center of local urban life throughout the intervening centuries.

As the Norris Square neighborhood of cottage industry and open space gardens, located to the north and east of Penn's original town plan, became a working-class factory neighborhood and later the "Badlands" of poverty and drug trafficking, Rittenhouse Square filled in with generous, upscale, residential-commercial buildings. Irrespective of class, trees were removed in both neighborhoods, and the mandate of "one green acre per five acres developed" was ceded to cobblestone, brick, and granite in Rittenhouse Square, and to brick, mortar, and asphalt in Norris Square. In each, only a park remained as the sole local remnant of the early greene countrie towne plan—*until the greening of the Norris Square neighborhood*. The community gardens express a new kind of urban renewal, one defined by beauty, nature, and culture coexisting, as they do in *Raices*. Like sidewalk cafes, the gardens restore outdoor life to city neighborhoods. Even bankers notice them, as highly visible harbingers of more costly, long-term housing rehabilitation and local economic development.

Project Rainbow

In a nearby neighborhood, Sister Diana Cerchio took the three- and four-year-olds of Project Rainbow, a residential program for homeless women and their children, down the elevator five floors from their lunchroom to the walled outdoor courtyard where they put their compostable leftovers from lunch in the worm box. "No meat, but eggshells and apple cores are okay," she reminded them, with an ease burnished by some thirty years of teaching. Carina pulled back a loose cover of hay and strips of newspaper to offer her apple core to a clump of plump red worms. Sister Diana lifted one side of a large, cylindrical planter so that Douglas and Hakeem could collect small, common red worms that are drawn to the dark puddle under the container. They added these to the worm box.

Sister Diana is a "master composter" trained by the City of Philadelphia's Recycling Office and the Penn State Extension Urban Gardening program. Having no local landfill, and with one million tons of garbage generated per year at the cost of seventy dollars per ton for disposal, and with two city incinerators at the center of citizens' lawsuits and an EPA investigation, Philadelphia was the first large city in the country to mandate recycling of paper, bottles, certain plastics, metal cans, and organic waste. Calculating that about 25 percent of weekly curbside trash is organic and compostable, the city began an innovative citywide program to train master composters in methods that range from passive piles of leaves, to mixing leaves and grass, to such singular ideas as worm farms for kitchen wastes.

Of all the options, a worm farm was ideal for the grassless, treeless container garden courtyard of Project Rainbow. Eight inches of shredded newspaper and hay provided the bedding into which red worms were added. The children cut their lunch waste into small pieces, because "worms have small mouths," and gently place it between layers of the bedding. In time, the organic material will be converted into nutrient-rich worm castings that the students will dig out and place in their garden containers. These children are practicing state-of-the-art urban environmentalism. In a country that generates more than two hundred million tons of solid waste per year, of which 15 to 25 percent is organic, compostable matter, only one percent is composted for reuse.

A medley of containers covered with salt marsh hay flank the beige brick courtyard walls of Project Rainbow: an ancient galvanized zinc washtub, a discarded rubber tire with a fluted outer edge, an oaken wine barrel enclosing a fig tree winter-wrapped in burlap, rectangular plywood boxes holding four milk crates lined with fine wire mesh, another plywood box punched with circular holes to hold pots of herbs. No one pot matches another, yet these assorted plant containers share a common history. Salvaged from the alleys and vacant lots of North Philadelphia, covered to keep alley cats from designating them litter boxes, they held last year's prize-winning garden: scarlet runner beans, sunflowers, marigolds, sweet potatoes, Red Norland potatoes, cherry tomatoes, early peas, various lettuces, radishes, carrots, onions, peppers, and herbs. Their luxuriance, variety, and plant culture won first place for "community children's gardens" in the 1993 annual City Gardens Contest sponsored by the Pennsylvania Horticulture Society. Above the worm box hangs a citation from the Horticulture Society:

> This container garden is located in the courtyard of Project Rainbow, a transitional housing program for homeless women and their children. The garden is planted and tended by 3 to 5 year old children who live at Project Rainbow under the loving instruction of Sister Diana Cerchio of Project Rainbow and Sister Maureen O'Hara of the Penn State Extension Urban Gardening Program.

One of the Rainbow Kids in courtyard garden.

IRA BECKOFF

Both Diana and Maureen live in Catholic communities of women that, like many religious women's communities during the past two decades, have reassessed and redefined their mission in the city. Project Rainbow, or the Drueding Center, as it is more formally known, was once a nursing home run by the Sisters of the Holy Redeemer. In 1987 the community conducted a survey of the neighborhood and determined that the people most in need of assistance were homeless women and children. Putting their considerable institutional acumen to the task of helping women free themselves from male violence and overcome low self-esteem, addiction, and dependency, the sisters have built a model program. Women who live at Rainbow enroll in a General Equivalency Degree program or in college, get technical skills or a job, and start a savings account toward the cost of moving into their own apartment. While they are studying and working, their children are enrolled in a fully licensed daycare program which is located on the fifth floor of the Drueding Center, and in which Sister Diana teaches.

Sister Maureen O'Hara can pinpoint this garden's beginnings: It was a morning in 1989 when she visited Rainbow wearing a t-shirt with the logo of Penn State's Urban Gardening Program—the Philadelphia skyline with plants growing through it. When the children pointed to a radish on her shirt and called it an apple, she said, "I knew they needed someone to work with them." Need is necessary, she added, but not sufficient for a community garden to work. In providing technical assistance for demonstration gardens in Philadelphia's low-income communities, she finds that the key ingredient of a successful community garden is "having someone who wants it—whether they know gardening or not." With kids, the former elementary school teacher pointed out, "there has to be at least one adult with interest to keep them interested. When kids are interested, they will keep learning." That person at Project Rainbow was Diana.

The two women began the children's garden across the street from the Drueding Center in a large two- to three-lot community garden organized by the Catholic Worker, a residential community that provides shelter and meals for the poor and homeless. They used milk crates for growing boxes so "we didn't have to teach kids where to walk." One child and his mother, Maureen recalled, weren't getting along; the child looked uncannily like his father, who had abused her. The mother had her own plot in the Catholic Worker garden, and the child, intrigued and stimulated by the seedlings, plants, and insects in his own milk crate garden, began learning language and number skills rapidly. The common bond of gardening lightened their tension and gave them some easy moments together; through that summer's growing season, "they learned to get along."

Capitalizing on Diana's expertise in early childhood education and her love of horticulture, Maureen decided to establish the Project Rainbow garden as a demonstration project for daycare workers in Philadelphia. The two women planned a container garden in the building's inner courtyard that children could tend all year round, with Maureen providing technical assistance and resources, and Diana doing the day-to-day guidance.

The garden year unfolds accordingly. After Christmas the children cut branches from the Christmas tree and lay them over their plant containers to deter cats. All winter they fill the bird feeder and add their compostable lunch scraps to the worm box. Inside they force spring bulbs and plant seeds, mark their growing pots with Diana's help, and start their seedlings under fluorescent grow lights in their learning room. Planting in the courtyard begins in late April and May, and they spend the summer mornings watering and watching their plants for the first blossoms, vegetables, and insects. Diana uses insects and plants as opportunities for teaching language, number, and nature skills. "Why is the ladybug a garden friend? How many dots are on her back? What are the colors of the hyacinth bean flower?" In July, a team of judges from the Horticulture Society visits to view their entry in the "community children's garden" category of the citywide contest. For the fall harvest the children and Diana make a scarecrow and decorate the courtyard with cornstalks from their garden. With herbs, they make potpourri for their mothers. The outdoor gardens close down for winter when what can be collected for storing or growing inside is garnered: seeds from marigolds, sunflowers, scarlet runner beans, and hyacinth beans are collected; dahlia bulbs are dug up so they can rest dormant in a dark place inside; cuttings from thunbergia, thyme, and oregano are placed on a windowsill in water or under the grow lights. During winter the Rainbow kids stroke the herbs, imitating Diana, to release their scent and summon last summer's courtyard garden.

The Rainbow courtyard is enclosed by multistory buildings that limit the hours of direct sun on the gardens. So in spring 1993 Maureen planted a Golden Muscat grapevine, a late grape that is harvested in early October, in a metal container on wheels that she found on the street. On wheels, the shopping basket planter can follow the sun, much as the Aztecs of Tenochtitlan propelled

FACING PAGE: *Container gardens and children in the Rainbow garden.*

their lakeside floating gardens with long poles to track the sun. With the children she built an arbor and trained the grapevine to climb it; strawberries carpet its base. "I always engage the kids in building and repairing the containers, even teaching them to drill holes. Unlike teenagers, little kids don't mind getting their hands dirty. I tell them that 'it holds life, and just like my life and your life it needs to be touched, *but gently*.'" Sounding much like Bernadette Cozart teaching respect for plants to her truant teenage gardeners ("This is not your football, it is not your basketball . . . You can't throw it in the closet. It's a living breathing thing."), Maureen instructs the children in care of soil. "You don't throw it. You touch it. If you ever have a chance to walk in the woods, walk slowly. It's a plush living carpet."

MARY VAN MUELKEN

"Gardens didn't come early to me. I grew up in a five-story apartment building in New York City. My first garden was at the Motherhouse," the central administration, infirmary, and home for retired sisters of her community located on 163 acres in Yardley, Pennsylvania. The garden was her refuge from the classroom. Maureen found the routine of teaching and then working in administration in elementary school deadening; she was restless, so she started gardening after school and on weekends. "My first garden was small but increased to twenty-three hundred square feet. I grew mainly vegetables—tomatoes, lettuce, and squash for the sixty to ninety sisters in the Motherhouse— and added flowers when I learned about their capacity for insect control." She was looking for an alternative to teaching, something with more diversity and stimulation, yet she didn't want to get another master's degree. She attended a session on horticultural therapy at Friends Hospital but was reluctant to pursue it because she didn't have a science background. A speaker at the program from the United States Department of Agriculture Urban Gardens Program at Penn State University encouraged her to apply for a job in that program, "and here I am."

"But it's one thing to garden; *it's another to cultivate the Earth.*" Sister O'Hara shuttled rapidly among the influences that have invigorated her spirituality: Ruth Stout's articles on soil in *Organic Gardening*; the pioneering work of Dr. Rosalie Bertell, a biophysicist in her community who exposed the human health hazards from nuclear weapons and nuclear power production; a trip to her ancestral Ireland; and a newfound Gaian strain of spirituality.

"The gardening was first, then my spirituality grew along with it. Everything we have on Earth comes from the Earth and it doesn't disappear." O'Hara referred to conversations with Bertell about the hazard of lead contamination in urban soils, in which they compared Bertell's findings around lead smelters with the levels of lead found in street dust and yard soil in North Philadelphia. In some cases, the levels were comparable. From Ruth Stout's writings she learned respect for the structure of soil, and came away with the conviction that the more you work the soil mechanically, the more you harm its texture. "When I first gardened, I used a rototiller, but no more. It's not the size of a garden but the quality of soil that matters to me. My goal is to grow more in less soil." She composts on-site with horse manure, leaves, and grass clippings, and brings in finished compost available to city gardeners from Fairmount Park in West Philadelphia.

A recent trip to Ireland with her family provided the cultural clue to the deeper appeal of gardening. "In Ireland I realized that cultivating the Earth is in my history, a collective memory carried within me. It is in everyone's history," she added, "everyone's ancestors were connected to the Earth."

For some city folks, like the Puerto Rican residents at Second and Dauphin Streets, where she developed a three-lot demonstration garden and composting project, the memory of gardening is fresh and beckoning. But the obstructions are colossal, including local cocaine rings and drug crime on the streets, and demolition waste and buried garbage on the garden site. Empty lots in poor neighborhoods are a minefield, O'Hara warns, illustrating with a vignette from local urban garbology: "When the city knocks down a house, the demolition waste is shoved into the open foundation. Often broken concrete from excavation sites is disposed there to fill in the cellar hole. Following the city's example, local people start tossing in tires, burying bags of garbage, and stripping cars in the lot." In the process of beginning a community garden on one of these vacant lots which had degenerated into local landfill, O'Hara has pulled out car batteries and syringes. She removes "anything that won't decompose." Exhumed glass and metal are recycled; wooden beams, bricks, and foundation stones salvaged from the original nineteenth-century factory housing are reused to frame gardens and walkways. Broken chunks of concrete and stone aggregate from sidewalks are mixed with a cementitious material and become boulder-like supports for raised herb beds. Three-foot earthen berms planted with flowering shrubs buffer the street side of her demonstration garden from car and truck fumes and lead-contaminated street dust. She builds raised beds with compost and manure from the Fairmount Park composting site to safeguard against lead-contaminated soil; and thorny vines climbing chain link fences deter vandals.

In late 1991 Rosalie Bertell gave Maureen O'Hara a copy of the proceedings of the World Women's Congress for a Healthy Planet. Fifteen hundred participants, including Bertell, had gathered from eighty-three countries to analyze the structural causes of worldwide environmental destruction, and to create a women's agenda for the upcoming United Nations Conference on Environment and Development in Rio de Janeiro. Women testified about the environmental impact of militarism, overconsumption, and nuclear weapons testing, and indicted systems of inequity that leave the poor with the most degraded and polluted land, water, and air. The Congress documented examples of women's reforestation and solar cooker projects in Africa, organic agriculture in Latin America, and green consumer activism in England and the United States, and called for community report cards with which citizens could grade their local community for the quality of its natural environment, human development goals, and social priorities. Sister O'Hara recognized the global pattern of economic and environmental inequity replicated in American inner cities, where the urban poor live in the most polluted and degraded environment. And she also saw community gardens as part of a worldwide environmental activism that joins tree planting in Kenya and wasteland restoration in India with organic vegetable gardens and composting in North Philadelphia. For a celebration of Earth Day in April 1992, O'Hara designed a logo that expresses her vision and mission in cultivating the Earth in Philadelphia's mainly African-American and Latino low-income communities. She split a graphic of the planet in two ("because that's what is happening to the Earth"), rejoined its polar ends, and turned it into a butterfly, an emblem of transformation. Her logo captures the passage of the neighborhoods in which she works, from moldering habitats to places of beauty and sources of community pride, through the instrument of community gardens and the political will of gardeners, nuns, and *motivos*.

USDA Urban Gardening Program

Perhaps the most significant benefit of community gardening is providing a piece of land for people to call their own for a season at least. It's estimated that more than 20 percent of U.S. land is held by corporations, much of it around cities and suburbs where the need for gardening space is acute. For landless Americans, community gardening can be the first step toward self-sufficiency—providing land to garden, a place to call "mine," and the opportunity to grow and produce things of value.

—Ishwarbhai C. Patel

The Penn State Urban Gardening Program, through which Maureen O'Hara has been setting up demonstration gardens such as the Rainbow children's container garden, and which trained and certified Diana Cerchio as a master composter, is administered by the United States Department of Agriculture Extension Service. The program began in fiscal year 1977 when $1.5 million was appropriated for the creation of urban gardening projects in six cities: New York, Chicago, Los Angeles, Philadelphia, Detroit, and Houston. Three criteria, in particular, shaped the choice of cities: size of population, number of low-income people, and that funds be limited to one city per state. In 1978 another ten cities were added and the funding was expanded to $3 million. By fiscal year 1989 the program included twenty-three cities in twenty-three states; but appropriations were only $3.5 million, due to no increase in funding in the first term of the Reagan Administration and the Gramm-Rudman-Hollings deficit reduction cuts in the later 1980s.

The mission of the urban gardening program is to assist low-income people in cities to grow and preserve food, thereby improving their nutrition. The twenty-three state programs submit annual reports to the USDA, which in turn reports to Congress. The key parameter of program success is a classical economic index: the return on investment, measured in produce grown. A USDA formula converts garden area, length of growing season, quality of produce, and distance between rows into the dollar value of production.

Dollar value of production	=	Area (sq. ft.)	x	Crop intensity* (distance between rows)	x	Crop quality	x	Length of Season (frost-free days)
						Good = 0.7		200 or more = 1.2
						Fair = 0.4		Less than 200 = 1.0

*Less than 1 ft. = 1.2   2 ft. to less than 3 ft. = 0.8
1 ft. to less than 2 ft. = 1.0   3 ft. or more = 0.7

Source: Ishwarbhai C. Patel: County Agricultural Agent, Urban Gardening, Rutgers Cooperative Extension, Newark, New Jersey.
Journal of Extension *(Winter 1991), p. 7.*

In 1985, every federal dollar invested in urban gardens yielded a return-in-food-produced of about six dollars. More remarkable is the return on investment to community gardeners. In 1989 the USDA Extension Service reported that almost two hundred thousand gardeners in the urban garden program, of whom 64 percent were minorities, produced an average equivalent of $115.70 each. Nearly eight hundred acres of "farmland" within the largest American cities were under cultivation that year. In 1992, low-income families in Philadelphia grew an average of $700 worth of produce per household plot, and realized a rate of return (in food produced) of seven dollars per one dollar invested. This 700 percent return on investment does not include the added benefits of growing and eating fresh vegetables and fruit with one's neighbors: health, exercise, a sense of community, enhanced property values, and crime deterrence.

Another less tangible benefit is the land ethic that community gardens offer the urban landless. Ethnobotanist Gary Paul Nabhan has observed that the success of certain Native American groups in conserving wild plants for centuries lies in the unity of their agriculture with human culture. Native American farming, passed on to children by their elders, is "grounded within a community fixed in place." Some similar harmony between plant cultivation and human habitation occurs in urban community gardens. The social fabric of inner cities is acutely weakened by the public neglect of inner cities, the flight of people and capital from cities, and the vulnerability of the poor to drug trafficking and its related crime. "What the gardens do is give us hope," said Florie Dotson, a community organizer and gardener in Philadelphia. Hope is stirred when corn rises from what was once rubble, raised by the hands of newly arrived agrarian people. Hope endures when gardeners become a community whose gathering place is "Hope Springs," "Enchanted Marston Gardens," "Five Star Garden," "Green Acres," "Roses of Roxbury," and "Garden of Eatin'."

The USDA Urban Gardening Program must rank among the most cost-effective of government programs, yet it has lain in the backwater of federal priorities. Even as its budget declined in real dollars since its inception, the program has grown in the number of cities served and the number of volunteers trained as master gardeners and master composters to work with urban gardeners, in the acreage cultivated and the yield of fresh produce per gardener, and in new educational initiatives such as hydroponics programs for youth. In 1989, thirty-two hundred volunteer master gardeners and composters in the USDA program worked with two hundred thousand low-income urban gardeners, the majority of whom were senior citizens and women of color. Together they produced $22.8 million worth of produce—all with a budget of $3.5 million! When the Rutgers, New Jersey Cooperative Extension surveyed its participating Newark and East Orange gardeners about what they needed in order to produce better gardens, the respondents gave as their priorities organic manure and leafmold, seeds and seedlings, permanent garden sites, rototilling, and guidance from program staff—not handouts, in other words, but the basic materials and services needed for self-determination and productivity.

The rural poor who have land of their own and the skills to work it live with an independence that is out of reach for the urban poor. The USDA Urban Gardening Program demonstrates that urban gardens can make the difference between utter dependence and a measure of independence for the urban poor. Setting out to measure the socioeconomic impact of community gardens, Dr. Ishwarbhai Patel, an Essex County agricultural agent, interviewed 178 gardeners in Newark, New Jersey. The respondents—mainly low-income, middle-aged and older African-American women—reported the benefits of healthy food, substantial money saved, and the sense of community, friendship, and reaching out to others that comes with community gardening. Listen to the urban gardeners polled by Patel: "I have hardly bought any vegetables since gardening;" "I garden mainly to save money and provide vegetables to meet our family's needs year-round;" "I plant varieties that I can't get at local markets or ones that are too costly;" "My harvest is fresh and doesn't cost me anything;" "Even people just passing felt like stopping and talking to gardeners;" "Over the garden, we knew who our neighbors are."

Terry Muschovic, director of the Penn State Urban Gardening Program in Philadelphia, stated that one of the most significant values of the community gardens is that "they are *safe* spaces for people in the city to come together. Gardens bring people together who might have stayed within their homes." However, neighborhood people's sense of safety has dramatically changed with the escalating drug trafficking. "Many seniors feel much more vulnerable and are more hesitant to be out, especially in the evening." Thus, the Penn State program can no longer hold evening meetings for the gardeners. Commenting on the greening of Norris Square, Muschovic characterized the neighborhood as having had the worst drug problems in the city and the largest areas of abandoned buildings and vacant lots. Norris Square was unique, she pointed out, in that business owners and residents made a concerted effort to organize neighborhood vigils with police to drive out drug trafficking, and began to turn the community around. As if echoing Tomasita Romero, one of Norris Square's garden leaders, and banker Don Haskin, she added, "But the neighborhood had no place to go but up."

Muschovic cited the involvement of competent and committed women as the key to Penn State Urban Gardening and Philadelphia Green—Ernesta Drinker Ballard, past president of the Pennsylvania Horticulture Society, Jane Pepper, the society's current president, and Libby Goldstein, the former director of the Penn State Urban Gardening Program, who hired Muschovic. They brought to the project financial acumen, a talent for institution-building, and a sense of mission, and achieved a rare, synergistic collaboration between the two organizations where competition might have interfered. These institutional underpinnings have made Philadelphia's citywide community gardening program a national model.

Ernesta Ballard had the vision of a citywide greening program in the early 1970s, created Philadelphia Green, and devised a way to fund it from the profits from the annual Philadelphia Flower Show, which she built into the most prominent show of its kind in the country. "She made the Pennsylvania Horticulture Society the society to belong to," Muschovic added. Her successor Jane Pepper has skillfully added major foundation and corporate funding to build Philadelphia Green into the largest and most esteemed urban community gardening program in the country. Libby Goldstein encouraged Philadelphia Green to pursue Community Development Block Grants from the city's Office of Housing and Community Development, since the Penn State program was not eligible for these funds. Meanwhile, she solidified her own program by appealing successfully to the state legislature for state funds to match the annual federal USDA budget. The two organizations then founded the Neighborhood Gardens Association, a citywide urban land trust to ensure the longevity and preservation of community garden spaces in Philadelphia.

Each institution uses its mandate to enhance joint projects. The Penn State program is obligated to spend its resources on gardening and horticulture education, and cannot provide materials such as fences, tools, soil, plants, and seeds. Philadelphia Green can provide physical and plant materials together with design and education assistance. Thus, the two programs worked together on an extensive garden site like *Las Parcelas*, with Philadelphia Green providing technical assistance, building and growing materials, and the Penn State program establishing a compost and garden demonstration project for adults and children. In the end community greening succeeds, Muschovic concluded, because gardening is a way of life for staff people working in the two programs, as well as for the community gardeners themselves. No one punches a time clock, and "we have a low level of bureaucracy and a low turnover of people." However, she observed, committed staff are not enough; "community gardens need community leaders like Iris Brown and Tomasita Romero in Norris Square, and Rachel Bagby in Susquehanna."

Susquehanna Greene Countrie Towne

Nineteen blocks west of *Las Parcelas*, in a neighborhood called Susquehanna, a handful of African-American retirees run the Philadelphia Community Rehabilitation Corporation, a nonprofit organization that rehabilitates housing, turns vacant lots into community gardens, and bedecks street corners with two-story murals. "This area of the city was left to fall apart," said executive director and founder Rachel Bagby as she explained how she got involved nearly fifteen years ago. "I saw a Planning Commission map in which this neighborhood was blacked out—didn't exist. Some people had lived here fifty or sixty years. I had an aunt here and I loved her. So I carried my complaint to the city. They wouldn't listen. I went to Washington. The federal government gave money and told the city to match." With neighbors she held cookouts and sponsored bus trips to raise money for a strategy and design session with the Philadelphia Architects Workshop. From that design session emerged the plan for the revitalization of Susquehanna.

But Rachel Bagby is not a housing developer. "They do houses. *I do lives,*" she said emphatically, contrasting her group with the city housing authority and other housing developers. "This whole world is skipping the kids and they're killing each other. We have almost lost two generations to dope, crime, and pregnancy." Asked where it started, she points unhesitatingly to the Vietnam War. "Men came back shell-shocked and full of dope. Came back and had lost their human feeling. Now we have babies having babies."

When Rachel Bagby first saw the escalation of urban and human ills in her extended neighborhood of Susquehanna, her own children were in school—a daughter at Stanford and two sons at Temple and Princeton. Once they were educated she retired from her job as a social worker for a non-profit housing agency, and "then I started." The city wants housing, she explained, "but just building housing is a band-aid. You can't just build housing for the community. You need a package for housing and *for education.*"

Rachel Bagby and Rose Lee Newsome.

Her package included getting mothers back in school, tutoring, and infant care ("that creates jobs, too"). The Community Rehabilitation Corporation has been trying to get a building for infant care so the mothers can go back to school. "As soon as the child knows the mother—that's about six weeks—it's time to educate." She paused and added thoughtfully, "It takes more money to work with two generations."

The people who preoccupy Bagby are those born into and growing up in a poverty that has deepened over the last twenty years, the families with children headed by a parent under thirty whose median income adjusted for inflation has declined by 32 percent since 1973, according to a recently released study by the National Research Council. They are single mothers with children whose incidence of poverty is seven to eight times higher than that of families headed by married couples. They are adolescents whose primary health care is fragmented and inadequate, who drop out of high school at a higher rate, who have no work skills, and who face futures of unemployment and further poverty. They live in zip code 19132, North Central Philadelphia, where the median price of housing in 1992 was $10,000, an increase of 43 percent since 1987.

Former Black Panther Elaine Brown grew up in this neighborhood. Her grandmother's narrow row house was wedged among hundreds of others into this yardless industrial-residential belt partitioned by the railroad, typical of Philadelphia's mid-nineteenth-century factory neighborhoods.

> Life did not seem a terrible affair just because my mother said so. I felt it. I felt it in the very house where I grew up. I felt it outside the house, out on York Street. York Street was buried in the heart of the black section of North Philadelphia. Its darkness and its smells of industrial dirt and poverty permeated and overwhelmed everything. There were always piles of trash and garbage in the street that never moved except by force of wind, and then only from one side of the street to the other. Overhead utility wires in disrepair ribboned the skyline. Cavernous sewage drains on the street corners spit forth their stench. Soot languished on the concrete walkways, on the steps and sides of the houses, and even in the air . . . Our house at 2051 was indistinguishable from the other grayish, two-story brick row houses on York Street. It was squeezed with the others into our block, a block no different in color from the rest of the neighborhood.

Edna Logan and her daughter at the vest-pocket garden.

The changes in Susquehanna since Brown's childhood there in the 1940s and early 1950s reflect the life and death struggle for neighborhood life going on in North Philadelphia. The expanse of barren factories, of windowless, wretched row houses, and cluttered and weedy vacant lots contrasts with Hagert Street, for example, a tree-lined street of freshly painted brick and stucco row houses whose corner is capped with a vest-pocket sitting garden and a two-story mural of a mountain waterfall. Edna Logan lives across from the waterfall; she rearranged her bedroom so that when she awakes "she looks out the window at it first thing every morning." Edna grew up here and credits a woman on Hagert Street, Dorsha Mason, whose stamina, sometimes "pain in the neck" pushiness, and stature among the neighbors have kept this neighborhood from drifting with the outgoing tide of dereliction and despair around them.

Dorsha Mason and Rachel Bagby are miracle workers, achieving feats of neighborhood planning and community building that confound professionals, "experts," and bureaucrats. With a hard-eyed realism Rachel Bagby observed, "the city gets money to fix poor neighborhoods but they ride around in Cadillacs and Mercedes. All us are volunteers—retirees, nine women, two men—with one paid staff." About their plans for financing more housing rehabilitation, she

said, "We'll work with any government that will help us. They would help us if they would just listen and let us tell them what we need. Now they're beginning to see."

Talking about gardens animated Rachel Bagby, whose large shovel and rake stood clean and burnished in a corner of the corporation's office, waiting for spring. Like Sister Maureen O'Hara, she found that that city kids don't know a sweet potato from a tomato. "Vegetables are harder to teach than flowers, especially the ones that grow underground." She illustrated the joint astonishment of mothers and children to find where food comes from:

> R.B.: "Potatoes grow underground."
> Mother and Child: "Potatoes grow underground, Miss Bagby?"
> R.B.: "Where do you get the milk from?"
> Child: "I get it from the store."
> R.B.: "Where does the store get it?"
> Child: "I think they get it from the truck."

Bagby added, "You get two generations by taking it from the ground to the table." She brought out her teaching aids—a large, sprouting sweet potato from last year's garden that she had wrapped in newspaper and stored in a cool, dark place all winter, and a section of sweet potato with leafy growth and a dense tangle of roots balanced by toothpicks in a jar of water. She will plant the sprouting tuber with children and their mothers in the three-lot Garden of Life children's garden on 20th Street, where she will pique their interest with the story of the sweet potato's life cycle, one that begins in last year's garden and finishes in a sweet potato pie at Thanksgiving—if they are good gardeners and keep the sweet potato patch watered and weeded.

Rachel Bagby came to Philadelphia from a farm in Columbia, South Carolina, and brought with her what she learned from her parents. "Others come here and become city slickers . . . They don't want to get their fingernails dirty or their clothes dirty. Don't want to kneel down and put their hands in dirt, and *they forget.* Gardens can put mothers and kids back in touch with the human side they've lost. Yes, as long as it's continued." At the children's garden on 20th Street, the Garden of Life, Bagby had the Philadelphia Anti-Graffiti Network paint the three-story corner building wall with images of children in the garden, children with strong bodies and large and luminous faces, some working the earth with hoe and shovel, others looking, curious and eager, onto the garden and from the garden out to the street. "So they could see themselves . . . it will transform them into human beings. *I know it can be done.*"

FACING PAGE:
Philadelphia
mural of
young people
in the garden.

Rachel Bagby has been too busy working to document the accomplishments of the Philadelphia Community Rehabilitation Corporation, whose ambitious but opaque name merely hints at the local social genius that has saved dozens of streets and corners of a major American city. Up the street from the Garden of Life and across from an elegant sitting garden is an entire block of handsomely rehabilitated two-story brick housing, which includes the Rachel Bagby Shared Housing, a shared living facility for senior citizens. On the wall of the corporation's spacious street-corner office is a series of prize ribbons from the Pennsylvania Horticulture Society's annual garden Harvest Show. Next to them hangs a map of the Susquehanna region with pins marking the corporation's housing and vacant lot restoration. It is years out of date because there has been "no time"—no time for glossy annual reports, for promotional brochures, for updating wall-size Planning Commission maps to showcase their achievements. On the cusp of eighty years, Rachel Bagby is fully aware that for her work to go on "it must be recorded." Could she, perhaps, walk around with a tape recorder when she's showing children how to plant sweet potatoes? "How can I," she exclaimed with a mix of humor and exasperation, "I need both hands for planting."

Women working in municipal housing and social service agencies drop by the office to consult with Rachel Bagby. They come for advice about bureaucratic obstacles, about policies and program decisions they disagree with,

Mae Burgis and the community flower/sitting garden.

about elitism and condescension toward poor black people, about how to make their agencies effective for the people of Susquehanna. Rachel Bagby tells them in no-nonsense fashion to work hard but not to lose their jobs. "Keep your mouth shut. Give me your complaints and let me work for you." After three women from city agencies left on one particular late March afternoon, she sat back at her long conference table and said, as if to the world at large, "I want it to go on. I want the change to begin now. I can't rest until change comes."

Philadelphia Mississippi

While Rachel Bagby's garden tools lay clean and polished for the oncoming season, gardeners of nearby Green Acres on Glenwood Avenue were itching to get out to their plots and start turning over soil. Tens of thousands of commuters and travelers have seen Green Acres in passing, without ever setting foot into North Philadelphia. This—Philadelphia's largest vegetable and flower community garden—is a source of amazement to Amtrak riders, who are otherwise numbed by the vista of crumbling factories and warehouses when suddenly they whiz by a four-acre farm. One hundred garden plots separated by white picket fences, a dozen tool sheds, a newly painted rust-red caboose, and dozens of red and blue 55-gallon water barrels interrupt, momentarily, the otherwise unrelieved industrial corridor along the Amtrak rail line that bifurcates this poor and working-class neighborhood of North Philadelphia.

Jimmie Taylor, the president of Green Acres, has always enjoyed the story of why this stretch of industrial-residential land is affectionately called "Philadelphia Mississippi." Sitting on his front porch, across Glenwood Avenue from Green Acres and the Amtrak line, he swept his arm in an arc to trace where warehouses had formerly occupied the garden site. "First there was whiskey aging in barrels, then a tire company took it over. There were fires all the time until the buildings were abandoned in the early 1980s." Taylor complained about the fires to the mayor's office regularly and worried about vandalism and arson in the vacated warehouses. Mayor Goode told him in early 1984, "Go home and sit on your porch . . . You're going to see wrecking cranes and bulldozers." He smiled and nodded, "Sure enough they came in June of that year." After the buildings were razed and cleared, leaving four bare acres with no fencing, Jimmie and his wife Ruth decided that if they didn't do something with the land, people would use it as a dump. "I suggested a community garden. She said, 'fine.'"

Ruth and Jimmie Taylor talked to a neighbor who suggested that they call Philadelphia Green. A staff person came that afternoon and discussed the resources that Philadelphia Green could provide. "You get me started," Jimmie told them, "and I'll do it." Philadelphia Green delivered fencing wire, and he and a friend put up the chain-link fence that surrounds the site. In time he designed and installed an ingenious water system. Pipes and hoses run from a hydrant on 18th Street, approved by the city for use by Green Acres, to spigots which fill 55-gallon drums located strategically throughout the four acres.

Ten years of assigning plots to would-be gardeners, of advising people on horticulture and garden care, of convening meetings and enforcing the rules of the Glenwood Avenue Green Garden Club, have given Jimmie Taylor a mother lode of opinion and insight. "The majority of people aren't crazy about nature. You got to be a lover of this stuff. It ain't enough to want a garden because Joe has a garden. You got to *love* nature." (He lingered on the o sound in *love* to make his point).

When Jimmie gives a plot to a new gardener, he does so on a trial basis for one year, and he claims he won't give a garden to someone in their twenties. "Young people who came up in the '70s are a waste . . . they walk the street all

Caboose donated by Amtrak, which serves as the Glenwood Green Acres "office."

Facing page: *Glenwood Green Acres.*

night . . . they steal your car. Kids born in the '60s, they're okay. It's when drugs started that the trouble started." Evidently the principle about not letting people in their twenties have plots is more absolute than his practice: two women who garden at Green Acres look to be no more than twenty-five. But Taylor makes the same desperate observation as Rachel Bagby—that in the 1970s drugs came in like a poison, infecting their young people and shattering their community.

On July 15, 1993, a team of judges from Philadelphia Green arrived to judge Green Acres in the annual City Gardens Contest. Jimmie Taylor was unperturbed about the contest criteria—variety of plants, horticultural practice, maintenance, use of space, imaginative ideas, design and total visual effect, suitability of plants, and community participation—as he led the team past mature gardens to a plot of newly emerging peanut plants. "This is my wife Ruth's plot. She died two months ago with a lot of seeds left to be planted. I planted the peanuts for her." Ruth had a reputation for being strict about maintenance of gardens. "She was plain spoken; if she had something to tell you, she said it. Like, 'I want this grass out of this garden,' to a gardener remiss in weeding. 'I don't want you to wait two to three weeks, *I want it out now.*' She would insult you and then make friends with you."

Willie Hawkins.

Ruth had two plots. The day she died, she had spent the morning planting flowers in her flower plot. Jimmie pointed to the young dog that played on his porch across the street. Ruth had found him newly born under one of the garden sheds; she brought him home and made him part of the family. "He took sick the day after she died—he was grievin' for her."

Jimmie Taylor prefers women gardeners to men, saying, "They take more responsibility. I put my wife on the men. Whatever she wanted done, she got it done." He prefers women to men among the staff of Philadelphia Green for the same reason. "Women get more done; they're more responsible for their jobs. Men aren't as involved in their job as women. You got to *love* this kind of work." He lingered again over *love*. "You got to be *into* it. You got to love anything you do. Like being a cook. I cooked for sixty years and I loved it."

Walking past plots of beans, eggplant, sweet potato, and staked tomatoes, Mr. Taylor introduced the team of judges to Willie Hawkins, who was turning under his "too tough" pole beans. "All that hard work and in one month down the drain," he said, referring to a month of drought and an eleven-day streak of record-breaking temperatures. He told about sitting by the window the night before "'til eleven o'clock," listening to the first rain in a month. "Now I know what the farmers went through. I love this work, anyway," he said, nodding toward his collard greens and black-eyed peas.

Two young gardeners came up to introduce themselves. Their energy blared it forth—they are the future of Green Acres. "What do we have to do to win first place?" Jeannette Rainey and Darlene Marcus asked the judges. "Our problem is getting out of third place and into second and first." Darlene explained that people get out in March to start their gardens and that by the time the judges come in July, many of them are clearing their first crops and starting another. "When we're in our prime, it's not the judging time," she lamented. She held out a copy of the recent newsletter that the two women published to show the judges their single-mindedness about winning first place.

Jimmie Taylor finished his tour of the gardens with the judges with a prideful tale about the reputation of Green Acres. "We had a lady from Britain stop by. 'We know what you're doing on the other side of the Atlantic,' she told me, referring to a British television show on the gardens."

The Heritage Eight

The elders of Glenwood Green Acres do not want their skills and their tradition to pass with them. In winter 1990, eight gardeners over sixty years of age from Green Acres began a dialogue at one of their monthly meetings that grew into the "Intergenerational Heritage Project." They share a common past: disciplined, hardworking childhoods on farms in the South with close ties to the land, then migration to Philadelphia to work in factories, warehouses, and "city jobs." In retirement, encouraged by Philadelphia's boom in urban gardens and the opening of Green Acres in 1984, they had a chance to revive early farming skills. In the spring of 1990, the Heritage Eight held a one-day workshop at Green Acres for forty children from the Busy Bee Garden, to share their heritage of planting techniques and history, especially for traditional crops like sweet potatoes, cotton, and peanuts, which had been passed down to them by their grandparents. They want to offer gardening to kids as an alternative to street life and television.

Alice Cooper told the Busy Bees that her whole generation in North Carolina was farmers and that "gardening and farming was a way of life and a way of survival." Showing her audience how to separate seed from cotton, she commented on the inefficiency of reaping machines. "Back then, there was no machine. This was the only machine." She held up her hands. "With machines, you can't do a second pickin' 'cause the machine destroys the plant. With your hands, you can go back maybe three times."

GLENWOOD AVENUE GREEN GARDEN CLUB

should have the following offices:

President: James Taylor, 1816 West Glenwood Avenue 229-7122

V. President: Lenard Sherrod, 1822 West Glenwood Avenue 223-0442

Co:Captain: Wilbur Hite, 2018 North Newcomb Street

Treasurer: Vennie Taylor, 1816 West Glenwood Avenue

ELECTION OF OFFICERS WILL BE EVERY TWO YEARS.

1. Duties of the President: To attend every meeting and be a member of Pennsylvania Horticultural Society. See about garden supplies by writing to different organizations. Get permission from the city to use the fire hydrant. Assign lots to each member. See that the garden is kept grass free, so that we can win first prize for the cleanest, most beautiful garden. If a spot is grassy it is up to the President to call a meeting. Next on the waiting list will have that spot. Appoint a committee to set up for a Harvest Table.

2. Duties of the V. President: Take over duties of the President when that person is out sick.

3. Duties of the Treasurer: President will give Treas. written orders when he wants money. Treas. should have a financial report at every meeting.

RULES

1. Each member must buy their own tools. Bring tools to garden and leave with tools.

2. Each member should make arrangements to have their spot broken up by May 31st of the garden year.

3. If the spot is not completely broken up by June 15th, the Pres. will call a meeting and request that the spot be taken away and given to next person on waiting list.

4. If a person should take sick and want to resign, they should submit a written notice to the Pres. or V. Pres. so the next one on the waiting list will be given the spot.

5. The Pres. is the only one that will be handing out spots to new members.

6. Members are permitted to bring friends to see their garden. Remember what you plant is what you are allowed to pick.

7. If two persons catch anyone stealing from someone elses garden, they are requested to bring the theft to the attention of the Pres. who will call a meeting and urge members to vote the person out, regardless of how good their spot may look.

8. If a member steals some produce from another persons gardens, and that person gets sick because of dangerous chemicals used, the Doctor Bill will be on the lazy person.

COMMUNITY GARDEN MEMBERSHIP GUIDE

1. All fees per year for all members to be used for garden expenses.

2. All gardens will have identification numbers, and will be uniform in size.

3. Stake and rope markings will be used, including convient walkways.

4. All garden space must be used (vegetables or flowers).

5. Each member shall maintain their gardens reasonably free of WEEDS ROCKS VINES AND GRASS including adjacent WALKWAY. After a five day notice, garden and/or walkway will be cleared for you and a $5.00 fee will be charged to you. ALL FEES must be paid by the end of the year (DEC. 31st) with a 30 day grace request, or your garden will be reassigned to someone else.

6. Any fund raising for garden shall benefit the members that participate only.

7. The garden gate will be open from 6:00 a.m. to 8:00 p.m. each day.

8. All dues must be paid by second TUESDAY IN AUGUST.

A SPIRIT OF TOGETHERNESS SHALL PREVAIL!

March 1993

From another member of the Heritage Eight, kids learned to till green manure crops into the earth, "giving back nourishment from where you got it." One man told lore about always planting three seeds in a hill, "one to push, one to pull, and one to come up." A woman recounted the day her grandfather "papa" took her aside and said, "I'm goin' to teach you how to grow somethin' and you'll never be hungry." And Alice Cooper described the sound of cultivating cotton with a hoe. "Zing, zong, zing, zong . . . now that's music. You could sing with it and you didn't even know you was workin'."

At the end of the day, the children talked about what they like best. One seemed to speak for all: "When you finish planting it and picking it, you get to eat it."

Philadelphia Green

Signs bolted to streetlight and telephone poles all over Susquehanna read "Susquehanna Greene Countrie Towne." The designation encompasses a hundred-block area in which color relieves pallor: blocks with half-barrels and window boxes brilliant with fluorescence, shaded by a canopy of street trees; blocks with assorted community gardens; small sitting gardens with three-story murals, benches, and wrought-iron fences; two- to four-lot intensive vegetable gardens; and mixed flower and vegetable gardens. The eye moves irresistibly, like a pollinating insect, from deep purple, rose-pink, and white petunias to the cerulean blue lobelias on sidewalks and sills, and finally alights on the lime, coral, and azure pastel fronts of the brick row houses. Nearby streets in all directions reveal the extraordinary energy that has enabled some pockets of Susquehanna to resist the social and physical entropy of North Philadelphia.

There is a bridge called Philadelphia Green that spans the chasm between Susquehanna Greene Countrie Towne and Society Hill, neighborhoods of Philadelphia that are physically proximate but metaphysically hemispheres apart. They are contrasts in black and white, poor and rich, etched in the city's past of private wealth-building and governance that benefited Society Hill and failed people of color. Philadelphia Green staff cross that bridge to bring fencing, soil, and trees to neighborhood garden clubs and block associations. And from time to time Rachel Bagby crosses in the opposite direction to attend an advisory board meeting of Philadelphia Green at Third and Walnut Streets — always in command of what's needed in her community. About the benches that Philadelphia Green provides for sitting gardens in Greene Countrie Townes,

Rachel Bagby says with her signature flintiness, "We gave 'em back and put in our own. Senior citizens can't sit in Philadelphia Green benches. When you sit, you can't get up."

The pressing questions about this bridge between Society Hill and North Philadelphia have to do with its purpose and function, with its structural integrity, with its traffic patterns. Who crosses it and why? Is it mainly a one-way "bridge of flowers" — the outgrowth of an institutionalized crusade of altruistic horticulture society ladies bringing flower boxes to the inner city? Is the flow mainly from the "haves" to the "have-nots"?

Ernesta Drinker Ballard was the architect of Philadelphia Green. She described its forerunner, the 1950s initiative of Louise Bush Brown, director of the Pennsylvania School of Horticulture for Women where Ballard studied. Any low-income block in which 85 percent of the residents agreed to plant and maintain the flowers for two years was provided contact with a garden club registered with the Neighborhood Gardens Association. Brigades of garden club women brought window boxes and petunias to North Philadelphia. And a small chain reaction ensued among the residents: window boxes led to clean-ups of vacant lots, yards, and streets.

Ballard, who was part of the Neighborhood Gardens Association, as the initiative was called, described it as having "the aura of Lady Bountiful." When Ballard became president of the Horticulture Society, she determined that the traditionally elite organization ought to engage in community outreach to low-income Philadelphia communities with a model of self-help and mutuality. She attributes the inspiration of Philadelphia Green to her feminism. "My feminism enabled me to understand racism. We took a different approach than the Neighborhood Gardens Association—not gardening as charity but helping people to help themselves."

Philadelphia Green started in 1974 with a staff of two and a budget of $25,000. J. Blaine Bonham, a portfolio manager for Pennsylvania National Bank, had taken Ernesta Ballard's course in horticulture for a diversion and began "madly growing plants." Ballard hired Bonham—who was restless and looking for more challenge in his work—to launch Philadelphia Green. Today he directs a staff of nearly forty people and a $3 million community gardening program that works with more than eleven hundred neighborhood groups, has sponsored more than two thousand greening programs, planted more than 925 trees in 1992, and is the largest comprehensive community greening program in the United States. Activities such as the City Gardens Contest and the Harvest Show, which award prizes for gardens and garden bounty, bring suburban and urban gardeners together in competitive and festive events. Funding for Philadelphia Green comes from a mix of public, private, and nonprofit sources, including the Pennsylvania Horticulture Society's Philadelphia Flower Show, Pew Charitable Trusts, the William Penn Foundation, and the City of Philadelphia.

"At its simplest," Bonham said, "it's just a gardening program" providing soil, trees, growing barrels, and technical advice to low-income communities in Philadelphia. As the program grew, so too did the options for neighborhood open space: picnic area, barbecue pit, orchard, sitting garden, and so on. On another level, "we are like midwives" for community people such as Jimmie and Ruth Taylor who had the idea, the energy, the discipline, the talent, and the network, yet who needed technical and material resources. "Our staff are intimately involved with the gardeners and great friendships have developed." He described the artistry and creativity that gardening nurtures in people, adding that this commonality—the artist in the gardener—links suburban and urban gardeners. The gardens, green spaces, and green blocks "symbolize a low-income neighborhood's claim that, like everyone else, they want beauty, peace, and growing things."

While the recovering banker prefers deliberating on the nonmaterial benefits of community gardens in North Philadelphia, such as turning a block into a neighborhood, building friendships and working partnerships among people who have been increasingly divided by differences of race, class, and the entrenched geography of prosperous white suburbs and impoverished black and Latino city centers, Bonham spoke convincingly of the gardens' potential for helping rebuild parts of the inner city. Philadelphia Green is teaming up with emerging community development programs to integrate provision for open space into plans for housing, child care facilities, and other economic development. Community gardens, he pointed out, are a practical land use solution for formerly dense, yardless factory neighborhoods such as Norris Square, where there are now more vacant lots than are needed for new housing development. Further, vacant lots are a financial drain on the city. Philadelphia has an inventory of fifteen thousand vacant lots, each costing an average of $3,000 to maintain annually. The Department of Licenses and Inspections funds Philadelphia Green to develop one hundred of these lots annually (the equivalent of about fifty gardens), and, with this one-time investment, avoids costly long-term maintenance.

Perhaps the ultimate value of the community greening movement in Philadelphia is that, according to Bonham, "as women like Florie Dotson and Rachel Bagby create a present for their community, they are also saving the future." Bonham quoted Florie Dotson, the organizer of community gardens in a neighborhood called Strawberry Mansion: "We want Strawberry Mansion to attract people back into the neighborhood." Like many American cities, the population of the city of Philadelphia—2.2 million post-World War II, 1.6 million now—is shrinking. "Parts of Philadelphia will become uninhabitable; but some will survive. In one hundred years when the suburbs have destroyed themselves with the ugly sprawl and banal strips of malls," Bonham forecast, "the viable parts of our cities where neighborhoods are thriving will be places like Strawberry Mansion."

Patricia Schrieber, who directs the Education Department of Philadelphia Green, told the story of the West Shore neighborhood in Southwest Philadelphia to show why this program has become a national model for using community gardens to spur community development.

> In the 1970s West Shore, a ten-block neighborhood, started with window boxes, then went to trees and vacant lots. Based on the "facelift," a housing network organization located there to rehabilitate housing. At the Greene Countrie Towne ribbon cutting ceremony for West Shore, a banker cited the power of gardens to symbolize civic pride and tenacity and to be a catalyst for investment in the community.

Schrieber has helped structure, systematize, and document the ambitious program of Greene Countrie Townes, of which Susquehanna was Philadelphia Green's fifth and Norris Square its eighth and most recent. A neighborhood petitions or is requested by Philadelphia Green to become a Greene Countrie Towne, and an extensive study of the neighborhood is then undertaken by Philadelphia Green staff with neighborhood leaders. Together they assess the land and housing, the greening needs and potential, the community interest, organizations, and leadership, over what may be a six-month period. At the end of this phase in the Susquehanna process, Philadelphia Green developed a three-year greening work plan and budget with key neighborhood block groups and community organizers, including Rachel Bagby. The program goals encompassed more than one hundred projects: vacant lots turned into children's vegetable and flower gardens and sitting gardens for elders; entire garden blocks beautified with flower boxes and barrels; street trees; and neighborhood-wide centerpiece sites with space for picnics, barbecues, and parties. On each block a neighborhood group was responsible for the project while Philadelphia Green provided overall design plans, excavation where necessary, educational materials and programs, fences, tools, and plant materials. Other organizations, including the Penn State Urban Gardening Program and the Philadelphia Anti-Graffiti Network, worked cooperatively with staff and community groups on gardens and murals. Philadelphia Green's expenditures in Susquehanna over the four-year project period, 1986 to 1990, were $675,000.

RIGHT AND FACING PAGE: *Different views of the Glenwood Court sitting garden.*

The brochure published by Philadelphia Green on Susquehanna Greene Countrie Towne documents the extraordinary achievements of this four-year effort, whose flagship gardens include Glenwood Green Acres, the Garden of Life and the Busy Bees, two children's gardens, and Diamond Acres with its mural of Mount Kilimanjaro and the plains beneath with herds of African animals. But Susquehanna's greatest resource, according to Patricia Schrieber, is its people. "Resource," from the Latin *resurgere*, originally meant to "rise" or "surge again," as in the Earth's capacity to restore itself. The bond between human and natural resources in Susquehanna Greene Countrie Towne is indissoluble: They *surge again* together. Schrieber wrote of this unity:

Many of the neighborhood's leaders . . . have held a vision for what people could achieve in their community. Besides fostering deep friendships among neighbors, Willie Mae Bullock says, "they have been turning negatives into positives. You really have to look much harder beyond the gardens and the tree-lined streets to see the devastation." According to Rachel Bagby, "Words cannot express the kind of impact the greening has had in our community. It means such a great deal—to smell the cool breeze, the freshness of the flowers, the fragrance of Mother Earth, right here in our own neighborhood." These women give voice to the sense of self-confidence and energy generated by the many signs of rebirth around the neighborhood.

Ernesta Ballard has become less sanguine about the restorative power of community gardens in inner cities and the capacity of the bridge called Philadelphia Green: "The gardens' potential was greater thirty years ago." Drugs, as she sees it, have undermined the community-building potential and empowerment that the urban community garden movement once had. "I don't know what the bridges are . . . and I don't see gardeners crossing them." She refers both to the deepening, hardening poverty of inner cities, and to the phenomenon of the wealthy superinsulating themselves from the poor. Speaking from her experience of fundraising for the Philadelphia Foundation, of which she is a board member, she observed: "People who have money do not want to get involved."

Gardens help horticulture enthusiasts transcend the chasm between rich and poor, black and white, she admitted, but then added that the City Gardens Contest was "the most difficult thing [I have] ever done." When she first proposed a contest for city gardens in which members of the Horticulture Society would form teams and judge the gardens, the board of the Horticulture Society and Blaine Bonham didn't think it would work. "'Which gardens?' they asked. 'Who would want to go into North Philadelphia?' It was slow in starting, but then it took off. Now it's hard to believe how difficult it was to get people to buy into the idea." But the bottom line is that, even with successful City Gardens Contests and Harvest Shows that bring suburban and urban people together as gardeners, "rich white people do not like poor black people."

Rachel Bagby, Iris Brown, and Jimmie Taylor know first-hand and live full-time with the social ruin and setbacks their communities have suffered from drug trafficking and drug-related crime. It has made their organizing efforts harder—Jimmie Taylor must carefully screen applicants for his plots. Rachel Bagby has to do *lives*, not houses. And Iris Brown can promise her students beauty and fresh vegetables, but not jobs after high school.

The bridges these gardeners cross, as they walk past smoldering ruins and moribund tenements to gardens called *hope*, *life*, and *enchanted*, span rigors and obstacles that most others—who only know North Philadelphia from the wholly negative view of it on the six o'clock news—haven't the fortitude to face. And what if the local news carried the City Gardens Contest conversation in which a young black ghetto gardener explained to a curious and somewhat awed white suburban judge how she grew her unblemished roses without pesticides? "We try to let nature do it. We don't even use plant food; we just water. Philadelphia Green tried to give us some insect spray, but we don't use it." Would the news commentator suggest that the Horticulture Society sponsor a Suburban Gardens Contest with inner-city organic gardeners judging suburban gardens for environmentally sound gardening techniques? (The average suburban homeowner uses a higher rate of pesticide on lawn and garden than commercial farmers do on farms.)

If the federal government launched the initiative *reinventing the city*, would the project directors seek out Iris Brown of Norris Square and Florie Dotson of Strawberry Mansion? Or would they a priori write off these city neighborhoods as derelict and has-been, as persistent pockets of poverty, of "low-income and no-income" people and nearly worthless buildings—the statistical urban underclass of the 1990 census? How can the federal government pennypinch the USDA urban gardening program—a model of social and environmental justice in twenty-three inner cities—and then puzzle over the increasing resemblance of our inner cities to third world countries?

Peggy Williams is one of a handful of young black women who have built Enchanted Marston Gardens, an extensive organic flower and rose garden, out of six "nasty" housing lots full of demolition waste, trash, and cars on Marston Street. "I had gotten out of North Philadelphia some years ago; but circumstances forced me back. I didn't want to live in North Philadelphia but this garden makes me want to stay. You can come with a book. You can come with

a problem and forget." This spacious, shaded neighborhood commons has both a contemplative and communal aspect. She described how they decorate "with spider webs, ghosts, and jack-o-lanterns on Halloween," and the neighborhood celebrates every holiday throughout the year in Enchanted Marston Gardens. She and fellow gardener Lorraine Harris explained their pride and sense of competence in using large garden equipment, a pride magnified by the dignity that their work has given their neighborhood. "Lots of us don't go places, don't see gardens. We call this our oasis."

If anything, the community gardens—"sown" with Ernesta Drinker Ballard's social idealism and acumen and sustained by people at work in their neighborhoods—are not a way out, for most who live there can't leave, and some don't want to, but a bridge *back to* a neighborhood they had nearly lost, back to hope, community, friendship, and pride. Peggy Williams and Lorraine Harris have created what academics and professionals call "place-attachment"—a "glue that binds people to place" and is characterized by drawing neighbors together as a community, lessening stress, crime, vandalism, and flight, and stimulating public involvement, self-governance, and altruistic behavior. Enchanted Marston Gardens at 2427–2437 Marston Street were dangerous, uninhabitable tracts that are now truly enchanted places. Peggy Williams's feelings upon creating a public garden for her neighborhood are testament to the capacity for urban renewal in community gardens: "I didn't want to live in North Philadelphia. This garden made me want to stay."

In *The Private City*, his social history of Philadelphia, Sam Bass Warner writes that the plight of poor people of color in this eldest of American cities, and throughout urban America, originated in a tradition of growth and development that he calls "privatism." By privatism he means a philosophy which locates personal happiness in individual liberties and the quest for wealth, and which finds community in the "union of . . . moneymaking, accumulating families." Privatism in municipal politics ensures that an open and thriving atmosphere is maintained for money-makers:

> The tradition of privatism has always meant that the cities of the
> United States depended for their wages, employment, and general
> prosperity upon the aggregate successes and failures of thousands of
> individual enterprises, not upon community action. It has also meant
> that the physical forms of American cities, their lots, houses, factories,

and streets have been the outcome of a real estate market of profit-seeking builders, land speculators and large investors. Finally, the tradition of privatism has meant that the local politics of American cities have depended for their actors, and a good deal of their subject matter, on the changing focus of men's private economic activities.

The failures of this model of relying upon private gain to create public good—slums, substandard schools, economic disinvestment in inner cities, and the poor of center cities—are then supposed to be picked up by philanthropy of the beneficiaries of privatism.

At first glance Philadelphia Green fits the profile of such philanthropic privatism—a charitable venture funded primarily by the elite Pennsylvania Horticulture Society's annual flower show and major Philadelphia foundations. The "haves" give of their surplus profits to the "have-nots," and in the process preserve the heritage of the city where their "forefathers" accumulated their wealth. Further, community gardens are a benevolent, feel-good, and democratizing charity, because the have-nots are more likely than the haves to bring indigenous knowledge from their agrarian past.

Thanks to her feminism—and to Ernesta Ballard's founding instinct that community gardening be mutual, not *noblesse oblige* charity—Philadelphia Green evolved beyond the privatist philanthropic model into that of a community-centered resource and partner for the inner-city neighborhoods of Philadelphia. Every dollar's worth of fence and soil that Philadelphia Green provided for Glenwood Green Acres was matched and multiplied by sweat equity, as Jimmie Taylor installed fencing with friends and Ruth Taylor organized, educated, and disciplined the hundred gardeners of Glenwood Green Acres. As they cultivate *badlands* into *goodlands* and build "lives not houses," the inner-city citizens of Philadelphia create credit-worthy neighborhoods and streets rich in beauty and pride where people want to stay. They take the raw materials of plants, fences, and tools, and turn them into the complex goods of Greene Countrie Townes.

The most enduring wealth-building of Philadelphia may be the productivity of its modest citizens, *motivos* who work to save the metropolitan region's heart—its inner center city. Yet the added value of Enchanted Marston Gardens to Marston Street will be reflected only minimally in the price of homes, and the gardeners do not take home a paycheck. If there are limits or imbalances in this partnership based on self-help and community empowerment, if the tradition of privatism lingers, it is because the rich do not value—in their economics—the equity of the poor. The Gross National Product is enhanced by the formal economy of agribusiness, by the demolition of neighborhoods and the construction of highways, but not by the informal garden economy of the urban poor, nor the sweat equity that turns four acres of rubble into one hundred productive gardens. Reknitting the fabric of life—traditionally the unpaid and undervalued work of women—is the philanthropy of Philadelphia's urban gardeners, an investment that may prove to be the city's most valuable asset.

CHICAGO:

Hortus in Urbe

PREVIOUS PAGE:
*Dan Underwood
at the orchard
site.*

The activity of restoring the place where both our bodies and spirits reside waits on nothing.
— Ken Dunn, "Turn A Lot Around" Resource Center, Chicago

IN SUMMER THE KIDS MEET DAN UNDERWOOD AT 9:00 EVERY WEEKDAY morning and some Saturdays in front of Schiller School, across from the Cabrini-Green public housing project. Underwood is the supervisor and these kids are the work crew of the market garden venture called Cabrini Greens. When they meet, he explains their assignments and in which garden they will work that day. If they are harvesting salad greens or young vegetables, they will work in the early morning and late afternoon, picking, rinsing, and packing their produce for same-day delivery to local restaurants. One morning in July 1994, Underwood and the children started work late because they had to first attend the funeral of an eleven-year-old girl who had been raped and killed, allegedly by her mother's boyfriend, in her Cabrini-Green apartment.

They are and aren't children, observed Alex Kotlowitz in his book *There Are No Children Here*, a chronicle of two young brothers living in a nearby Chicago Housing Authority project, the Henry Horner Homes. Even coming into the world is more risky here: black infants in Chicago die at nearly three times the rate of white infants. One out of every three children in this city grows up in poverty, and 40 percent don't graduate from high school. These children of the other America are clustered in high-rise projects like Cabrini-Green that have become permanent warehouses for the poor.

By the time they are twelve and thirteen, many children in the city's nineteen public housing complexes have witnessed tragedy and terror that we associate with war in remote parts of the world, and they have felt the fear and trauma that those who live through wars do. They witness death and hear recurrent gunshots, fighting, and yelling; many are pressured and forced by older boys and men to join gangs, to buy and sell drugs, to brandish guns, to have sex and babies, and accordingly grow up with distorted messages of manhood and womanhood. "Despite all they have seen and done," wrote Kotlowitz, who spent two years meticulously documenting the embattled lives of Pharaoh, Lafeyette, and their mother LaJoe, "they are . . . still children."

That's what matters most to Dan Underwood—children. Whatever interests his kids interests him. He serves on the school council of Schiller School, where two of them are enrolled "because the public schools are terrible;" he

View of the Chicago River from the orchard site.

coaches the marching drum corps and the citywide champion jump rope team on which his fifteen-year-old daughter competes; he takes a troop of girl and boy Explorer scouts camping every year to Camp Owasippee near Muskegan, Michigan, where they learn to identify edible plants so "they don't have to kill anything to survive." In mid-July 1994, Jack Davis, the founder of Cabrini Greens, told Dan that he had finally secured funding for his salary. After more than a year of volunteering, Underwood became the full-time, paid supervisor of the day-to-day garden activities. With or without money, Dan says adamantly, he would be there.

He has plans to take the gardeners and Explorers camping in an apple orchard at the Heritage Farm of the Seed Savers Exchange in Iowa—part of his strategy to whet their enthusiasm for planting an apple orchard with heirloom and local varieties provided by Seed Savers. Dan has picked out an orchard site: a scraped-bare patch of land with overgrown edges along the Chicago River, not far from Cabrini-Green. There's an in-between cast to the surrounding area. One can imagine a vibrant commercial past in the strings of converging railways and clusters of vacant brick warehouses nearby. One can foresee a vibrant future for this urban riverfront, as well, crisscrossed with bridges all the way to downtown, where high-rise towers litter the horizon. On nearby streets, renovated warehouses are emblazoned with signs advertising loft and office space; and

ChicagoRivers, a consortium of agencies and non-profit organizations, has committed to cleaning up the Chicago River and making it a community asset. Dan is unclear about who owns the orchard site land (he thinks maybe the railroad); but he hopes the Cabrini Greens could lease it long-term before redevelopment along the river makes it too expensive.

Despite their fear of violence, Dan and his wife Annette recently moved with their ten children into Cabrini-Green. "We were blessed. We didn't always live in Cabrini. We lived on the West Side but the rent was high and we couldn't buy stuff for the kids." When he suggested moving into the housing project, his wife said, "No, they be killing kids there." He talked her into it because the low rent would enable them to send two of their older children to private high schools. One day in 1993 a few of his kids, who were playing basketball at the New City YMCA, came home talking about a flower garden at the Y which was part of a project called Cabrini Greens that they wanted to join. Dan inquired, and was asked to volunteer for the garden project. Now it's a life commitment: "As long as the kids come out for gardening, I'll be there."

A Day in the Life of Cabrini Greens

Dan and his crew of eight girls and one boy, ages ten to fifteen, spent the morning of July 20, 1994 weeding their half-acre tomato and mixed pepper garden and repairing broken and trampled fences around the site. The garden was planted on a generous plot of land behind a senior housing facility operated by the Chicago Housing Authority (CHA). Although the fences are the property of the CHA, Dan can't rely on the agency to repair them. In the afternoon he picked up a small crew of boys from the morning summer school classes to finish repairing the fences with him.

Earlier in the week the girls had installed fifteen hundred wire cages around the tomato plants that they and the boys had planted some weeks ago. This crop is their main late summer cash crop; the kids will share in the profits from their sale to top-dollar-paying downtown restaurants, including Charlie Trotter's, Frontera Grill, and Michael Jordan's. These restaurants bought the early summer crop of organically-grown Burpee gourmet lettuce mix, and will buy as many organic tomatoes and peppers as the kids can grow and harvest. A smaller portion of the garden is dedicated to white potatoes. The C.J. Vitner Company donated seed potatoes with the promise to buy their harvest for making potato chips, which the company will distribute locally.

The morning's work on July 20 looked straightforward enough—weeding and some fence repair; but the day's events were labyrinthine and obstacle-laden, like their inner-city lives. Just as Underwood and the kids were ready to leave their rendezvous point at Schiller School to work in the tomato garden, a teacher chased an eight-year-old boy who had called her "bitch" out the door of the school. Dan pursued the boy, who tore through one of their market gardens on Cabrini-Green land, caught him, and brought him back squealing. Teachers and kids gathered around while Dan called the boy's mother and the police. The boy's mother came almost instantly, yelled at him, and told him to go home. A few minutes later the boy's father ran over from Cabrini-Green cursing and threatening Dan for grabbing his son. A shouting match ensued; the scent of violence hung in the air like the morning's heavy, humid heat. Dan outshouted the father, and the teachers shouted above the two men, backing up Dan's rendition. The kids were excited but tense; they alternately laughed, cheered, and looked anxious. Eventually the teacher's story prevailed. Seeing he was outnumbered, the father turned sharply to the child, yelled at him, and poked him to go home. The police arrived just as the crowd dispersed.

As Dan and the kids got into his van to head for the garden, he said that the man who had threatened him is most likely a member of one of the gangs at Cabrini-Green, which is why he always calls the parents and "his gang"—the police—in situations like this one. Most residents in the housing projects distinguish between police who get to know the community, like the two women officers assigned to the four local schools, and those they loathe and fear—the ones on the take, the ones who will shoot without probable cause.

The tomato garden is a few miles away on the West Side, not an ideal situation, because it's too small a plot and too far from Cabrini-Green, but it's the best they have so far. Dan Underwood and Jack Davis are always on the lookout for land; one of their hobbies is riding around the city doing a windshield survey of unused or vacant urban land. Their preference is housing authority land, parks department land, corporate land, and vacant building lots, in that order. Ideally they would like to have twenty acres and work with a few hundred kids, although they admit that they would have to go to the suburbs for that extent of land. (Both men are willing, but they have different plans for organizing a suburban farm.) Even two contiguous acres in the city would do. Right now they have five quarter- to half-acre plots, with a few more available; most are on CHA land, two are at Cabrini-Green.

The topsoil on CHA properties is a rich, black, silty to clayey loam that only needs an initial plowing to be ready for planting. The soil initially brought in to Cabrini-Green by the housing authority for landscaping (a euphemism for the broad, drab, crabgrass and dirt aprons around high-rise public housing) may have been scraped from the fertile, loessal plains of the Midwest. By contrast, a vacant building lot may require five to ten thousand dollars' worth of excavation to remove buried building debris and chunks of blacktop or concrete, after which the soil must be rebuilt with manure, compost, and topsoil before it is plantable. Jack Davis will tell you that his soil samples from Cabrini-Green show little contamination with metals, good pH, and high organic matter. And the gardens yield healthy, organically-grown, market-quality vegetables, some of the best that he buys, according to Chicago chef-restauranteur, Charlie Trotter.

En route to the tomato garden, the kids took turns citing what they liked best about gardening: "digging, planting seedlings, and watching them grow;" "learning how many inches deep you have to plant the plants, how far apart they go, and how long they take to grow;" "planting pretty things;" "earning money, earning money, earning money, in that order;" and "having something to do

Girls working in the tomato garden.

over the summer." None of them had any enthusiasm for weeding, though; and after a few hours realigning the tomato cages they had installed the day before and pulling crab grass and jimson weed from around their tomatoes and peppers, the girls drifted out of the field — "tired of weeding," "tired from putting in tomato cages all day yesterday," but not too tired to do some exhibition jump rope. One, Khalilah, was a city champ; another, Ramona, was just joining the team. (Dan, the coach, said that he could tell, simply by hearing Ramona jump while he was repairing a fence around the tomato garden, that she had talent.)

Children growing market garden tomatoes where seniors live has been a boon for both groups. But before they had planted a single tomato seedling, Jack and Dan walked through the CHA's bureaucracy to secure permission to farm the land, then worked to win the approval of the president of the tenants' council. (The latter came easily, both men attested; the former might possibly have been fruitless, they said, were it not for a cooperative CHA garden coordinator named Tim Goosby.) In return for the tenants' council agreement, they tilled plots for seniors, and the children planted seeds and seedlings for seniors who could not plant their own. The seniors and staff, in their turn, kept a watchful eye on the garden, correcting children if they ended up throwing rotten tomatoes at each other, but also looking out for vandals.

A security guard and maintenance person told Dan who had overturned a few dozen tomato cages the night before: two local boys who had wanted to be hired for the garden project. (Dan had told them that he would first have to meet their parents, because he hires by the parents' attitudes as well as the child's.) The security guard told Dan where the boys lived, and he intended to talk with them and their parents to nip their vandalism in the bud. A girl leaned out the window of her grandmother's apartment, looking curiously and a little longingly at the girls weeding around their vegetables and then jumping rope. She is often at the window when the girls' crew arrives — a harbinger of this project's magnetism for children.

On the way back to Cabrini-Green after the morning's weeding and fence repair, Dan drove the kids through neighborhoods where fields of wild grasses and flowers have reclaimed former building lots. This windshield search for arable city land is reminiscent of more leisured peoples' Sunday drives on scenic country roads — even the wayside wildflowers are the same — except that in the inner city, one may have to negotiate with the street authorities. Dan stopped to inspect one expansive site ablaze with sky blue chicory, tansy, grasses, broadleaf

Watering marigolds.

HARLEM

ABOVE:
*Afro-Asian
Friendship
Garden at
Mary McLeod
Bethune
School, PS 92.*

RIGHT:
*Bamboo water
wheel in the
Afro-Asian
Friendship
Garden.*

HARLEM

Fourth graders in Building Blocks Playground and Garden at PS 197.

HARLEM

ABOVE:
Mural at the Garden Project.

RIGHT:
Students picking flowers at the Garden Project.

SAN FRANCISOCO

Above:
*Mural at the
Garden Project.*

Left:
*Students and
"stars" at the
Garden Project.*

San Francisco

BELOW:
*Mural
depicting
Puerto Rican
history and
ecology, in
Raices garden,
Norris Square
Greene
Countrie
Towne.*

PHILADELPHIA

IRA BECKOFF

ABOVE:
La Casita.

LEFT:
*Rose Lee
Newsome and
family mural.*

PHILADELPHIA

RIGHT:
*Presley
Robinson, Jr.'s
flower garden.*

BELOW:
*Willie Glaspy
taking a break
in the garden
at the Thomas
Flannery
Apartments for
Senior
Citizens.*

CHICAGO

Girls jumping rope after working.

Dan and his son mending fences.

plaintain and chamomile, and posted as CHA property. A man and a few women hanging out at one corner approached him and asked warily what he was doing. When he explained and gestured toward the kids in the van, they pressed for more information. Would anyone from the neighborhood be hired in a garden at this site? Would they sell vegetables in the neighborhood? When Dan answered yes, they warmed to the idea of market gardens in their neighborhood. The man pointed out other parts of the neighborhood where there was vacant land and shook hands with Dan when the discussion ended. They aren't the CHA, nor the tenants' council; but the message was clear that they—the man, in particular—ran that street.

As the garden crew arrived back at Schiller, they noticed a team of kids playing baseball in their trial purple potato garden, one of two market gardens on Cabrini-Green land, and the same one the eight-year-old had run through that morning. Dan jumped from the van, evicted the kids with speed and skill (but not without one angry boy trampling some plants as he exited), and then talked calmly with their coach. He explained the garden project, pointed out the potato plot that the outfielders were standing in, and gestured to the baseball diamond next to Schiller School, suggesting they practice there. The suggestion was reasonable, the coach agreed; they shook hands, and thus ended a workday for Cabrini Greens.

Child rests between the garden and playground at Cabrini-Green.

126

Dan Underwood knows these burdened neighborhoods with the clear-eyed wisdom of someone who grew up in them and is neither their victim nor their bully; his love is a tough, compassionate shelter for children. His solution to vandals in the garden is to plant extra vegetables and to rely on the vigilant eyes of the seniors, security guards, maintenance people, and teachers whose respect he has garnered. He shows no bitterness, no trace of frustration as he repairs the CHA fencing around the garden, fully aware that fences are the agency's property and responsibility, but also their lowest priority. He wants use of their land. He intervenes judiciously in wrongdoing and calls parents and police to settle disputes.

He pointed to nearby Division Street and explained how, when he was growing up in the early 1950s, one side was black and the other side was Italian. Then all the whites moved out when blacks started moving across Division Street. Houses became vacant, fell into disrepair, and were demolished to build Cabrini-Green. At one time, when his mother lived there, Cabrini-Green was a place where poor people could live comfortably and have a chance to save money and maybe buy a home. Now, a third and fourth generation of poor are still living there, stuck in this unsafe, perpetual slum. Why? Public housing built in the 1950s and 1960s was supposed to provide an alternative to substandard living conditions of the poor in slums. Instead, the new

Children playing ball at Cabrini-Green.

public housing—not wanted anywhere—was sited at the edges of black ghettos in powerless, voiceless political districts. It anchored already existing slums and devolved over time into new high-rise, high-density slums isolated from the rest of the city.

Poverty persists here for reasons that begin with ill-managed, deteriorating, often dangerous housing in which tenants expend most of their energies trying to survive. The reasons extend to inferior local public schools and the lack of local jobs. Children's playground areas at Cabrini-Green are ill-kept, monotonous stretches of blacktop or concrete littered with broken, aging playground equipment. Such negligence, with its message that slums and slum dwellers are nothing but disposable waste, can maim a child's desire to overcome being poor and dependent.

In the late 1980s the building structure of nearby Henry Horner Homes was of such low quality that elevator cables froze in winter, and people could break into an apartment merely by removing the medicine cabinet in an adjacent apartment. Building and grounds maintenance was so negligent that human waste has backed up into apartments, and dead animals have accumulated in basements—the same basements that, when the buildings were new, were used for dances and roller skating parties. The odor of the putrefying bodies of cats, dogs, mice, and rats has entered apartments through the plumbing systems. The educational system in ghettos was and still is rotten: In the early 1980s then-Secretary of Education William Bennett cited Chicago's public school system as the worst in the country.

Drugs came in like an affliction that resists any cure in the early 1970s; now young men prop up their manhood in gangs that control whole buildings in housing projects. Vacant apartments are taken over for drug operations; snipers from gangs have positioned themselves at the top floors of Cabrini-Green. In 1981 Mayor Jane Byrne moved from her Gold Coast apartment into Cabrini-Green and stayed for three weeks, with a cadre of police and bodyguards, in an effort to restore order. In the previous two months eleven people had been killed and thirty-seven wounded there.

On the same July day that the Cabrini Greens crew was weeding their tomato garden, armed gang members banished four unarmed Black Muslim security guards from two high-rise buildings at Rockwell Gardens, a CHA public housing complex on the West Side. The gang members locked the building doors, turned off the lights, and fired at a CHA police car. While the main dispute was between two rival gangs, sniper fire around the buildings held tenants hostage in their apartments until the CHA police and the unarmed security guards could restore order.

Dan Underwood cited the assassination of Martin Luther King and the release of the movie *Superfly*, which glorified the image of pimps in big cars and the high-living lifestyle financed by money from drug trafficking, as pivotal to the self-destruction of projects like Cabrini-Green. "Poor people do not import drugs," he said adamantly, referring to the belief of many that outside agents, including government, have used an abundant supply of narcotics as a means of anesthetizing rage and shutting down rebellion in ghettos. Black-on-black violence—which emerged as a morbid consequence of the drug business in ghettos—embattles a community from within and subverts and weakens its activism. Underwood continued, "a kid fourteen or fifteen years old selling drugs on the corner—he's all but dead. He's on his way to the penitentiary or the grave." The more young black men and women—who now make up the fastest growing jail population—that get killed or end up in jail, the fewer there are to build a new civil rights movement, whether it be based on community gardens and environmental justice, as in the work of Bernadette Cozart and Cathrine Sneed, or math literacy, as promoted by former Mississippi Freedom School teacher Bob Moses, or on community development and "streets of hope," built by the multiracial Dudley Street Neighborhood Initiative in Roxbury, Massachusetts.

Asked what was the major influence on his life, Underwood points to the Civil Rights Movement. "When I was seventeen, I joined and marched all over the South with Dr. King. I got to see him and hear him up close." He described seeing him through the crack of a door in Wisconsin: "Dr. King was sitting in his hotel room planning a speech and there was like a halo around him. When he was assassinated, I was young and full of rage. I was drawn to the Black Panthers . . . I should have been security for Martin Luther King." He said this last wistfully, as if he might have been able to save King, or at least have had the chance to try. This gardener/teacher/coach/surrogate father has never left the cause of peace, justice, and love. "That's where I am still, only now I teach children, I raise the children I teach . . . The way I see the garden is that it's a place to grow. We're not just growing vegetables, we're growing kids," he said, echoing Cathrine Sneed, who described the Tree Corps in San Francisco as planting trees *and* people. Money, says Sneed, can buy and re-

claim degraded land and preserve it in trust; but it takes a lot of love and hard work, as well as money, to reclaim discarded and degraded human beings and to rebuild human trust.

"Kids need certain things to grow just like plants need fertile soil and the right kind of light." Underwood illustrated his point with the story of Ramona, one of his thirteen-year-old gardeners. "I saw her out on the street at 11:30 one night, rolling around on the concrete, laughing, having a ball. I stopped my van, made her get in, took her to her home. But I quickly saw that I was more concerned for her than her family was." So he asked his daughter Khalilah, also a gardener, to spend more time with Ramona. "But my daughter didn't want to because Mona is too boy-crazy. I'm still trying to find a mentor for the child because she's still not out of the woods."

The incident with Mona illustrates the two sides to Cabrini Greens. Jack Davis envisions twenty acres in the suburbs where four hundred kids can learn how to run a financially successful market garden. Dan Underwood wants twenty acres, too; but he would like to build a residential facility there, where the kids could live safely, in peace, learn life skills, and also learn how to run a market garden. Underwood explains, "We're a business; but there's the educational side of this, the nonprofit side. The two sides need each other. There's the profit side, that's Jack; and the not-for-profit side, that's me."

The Profit Side

Jack Davis is an unlikely urban gardener: He doesn't like cities, he prefers small towns. He grew up in central Illinois and lives now in a suburb of Chicago only because his job as marketing director for an accounting firm brought him there. He explained how he conceived of Cabrini Greens and why he started the Inner-City-Horticulture Foundation, the nonprofit arm of the market garden; but his reasons did not compute into a neat social idealist's formula. First, he dispelled any expectations that he is softhearted or a political liberal. "Most media are looking for a warm and fuzzy story. I'm not a communist; I'm a Republican. The gap between rich and poor is increasing. There will be an insurrection in fifteen years if nothing happens. The key is education. The only capital these kids have is time." He delivered one-liners like Ross Perot. "What's the one thing money can't buy?" he quipped. "Poverty."

Many professionals who come into the city for work, like Jack Davis, also note Chicago's plight: the exodus of industry, capital, and the middle class; the shrinking tax base and the deteriorating physical infrastructure. Their face-to-face experience of urban poverty comes from passing more and more homeless panhandling on the streets of downtown Chicago; Cabrini-Green they only know, second-hand, from crime reports on the local news. Some resort to rationalizations of the "underclass" and "persistent poverty" to explain why poor people stay poor; in other words, that poor people reproduce and perpetuate their own poverty. This victim-blaming analysis is bolstered by the resurgence of genetics-based explanations (among psychologists, not geneticists) for why the poor are poor: that intelligence is gene-based and measured by IQ, that poor people and their children have lower IQs and, therefore, are intellectually inferior to the middle class and incapable of upward mobility. Many people simply accept, without first-hand knowledge, the view of places like Cabrini-Green that they see on the local nightly news and in the metro section of the *Chicago Sun-Times* and the *Chicago Tribune* — a view that narrows in on gang- and drug-related crime but rarely probes the deeper questions of cause or agency. Questions such as: Who started and who fuels the traffic in drugs and weapons in

FACING PAGE:
Dan explaining the Cabrini Greens project to a teacher and her students.

ghettos? Why isn't there more investment in local public schools and employment if politicians believe—as they state—that education and work are the keys that open doors out of poverty?

Like Jack Davis, a lot of people who work in the city and live in the suburbs garden as a hobby; it is the most popular avocation in the United States. For few, however, do the two—working in the city and enjoying gardening—add up to the formidable commitment demonstrated by Davis when he founded the Inner-City-Horticulture Foundation and approached CHA with the idea of farming their land with kids who live in Cabrini-Green. The answer to the question of why a self-proclaimed conservative who prefers towns to cities started Cabrini Greens is elusive. What's evident is that he has enormous energy and commitment; he likes the kids and respects Dan Underwood. He brings business acumen—a scarce resource—to Cabrini Greens, and he is clear-eyed about the consequences of the increasing gap between rich and poor. "Dan has got to get more businesslike," Jack said good good-naturedly. But he was also serious. If Dan were part of the conversation, he would chide Jack to "take care of business" and let him "take care of the babies."

Cabrini-Green is a stone's throw from the Loop, a long walk or short bus ride away from the Magnificent Mile; former mayor Jane Byrne had to come only eight blocks when she moved into the project to dramatize an epidemic of shooting and killing there. Yet this prison for the poor is another Chicago in another America that few leave and that few enter from the outside. Once in a while kids do leave to find odd jobs on nearby streets. It was a child from Cabrini-Green, shining shoes on the street in downtown Chicago, who first caught Jack Davis's attention and imagination.

As a child, Davis mowed lawns, until "a brilliant high school teacher whose lawn I mowed challenged me to grow beautiful roses." In the mid-1980s he started farming ten acres his father owned in Lewistown, Illinois. "I bought a $2000 Troybilt, and the accountant in me wanted to make it pay for itself. So I started growing elephant garlic. The first year it failed, the second year it worked." He sold his harvest to the best restaurants in Peoria to pay for his rototiller. A restaurant owner introduced him to the most lucrative produce to market: young vegetables and mixed salad greens. When Davis relocated to Chicago for work in 1990, he wanted to continue his longtime avocation.

One evening as he was leaving a business dinner at a restaurant in downtown Chicago, a young boy asked if he wanted his shoes shined. Davis agreed, "found

132

him really nice," and asked where he lived. The boy told him Cabrini-Green. Davis inquired whether there was a lot of land around Cabrini-Green. When the child answered yes, the idea of teaching kids like this one to grow gourmet vegetables for sale to upscale restaurants came to Davis "in a flash." He "decided to check out the land at Cabrini-Green." (He, like most others, knew the project solely by its crime profile.) Upon seeing the wide, rectangular swaths of contiguous land around Cabrini-Green, he immediately decided that a market garden on the housing project grounds, which could teach kids entrepreneurial skills, would simultaneously satisfy his yen for gardening and for doing something about the worsening inner city. The name, Cabrini Greens, announced itself in a second flash.

Davis is a single-issue person when it comes to this undertaking, arguing that if you teach and pay kids to work who might never otherwise have had a chance to *learn how to work*, if you "teach the work ethic," you can dispel the miasma of the ghetto. He proceeded to build the project systematically. He went to Tim Goosby, the gardening coordinator of CHA, for permission to use the land; then he got the approval of Cabrini-Green's Resident Housing Association, thanks to the lobbying of Thelma Ruffin, the association's chair. And he

Gourmet salad-greens garden at Cabrini-Green.

applied the same financial methodology he uses for customers at the Edwin C. Sigel, Ltd. accounting firm to Cabrini Greens: He wrote a business plan.

In spring 1991, Davis and a small band of Cabrini-Green kids rototilled a half-acre plot—ironically, it had better pH than his own garden soil in Lewistown—and grew about eight hundred dollars worth of lettuce, beets, onions, leeks, and squash flowers. Anyone who showed up was put to work, and they got paid at the end of the week for the hours they put in. He met kids and volunteers after work and on weekends, putting in twenty to forty hours per week during the growing and harvesting season. "It's really a simple concept, just a garden and a cottage industry for a very big cottage," Davis is wont to say. He knew marketing, he knew gardening, and he believed—in the face of others' skepticism—that kids could and would learn how to garden and sell their produce, especially if they were paid. The variable that surprised him was the quality of the soil and the vegetables it yielded. Local restauranteurs have praised the outstanding quality of their produce.

The Market Plan

Eight hundred dollars for a harvest is a fraction of what Davis projects in his economic development plan for Cabrini Greens: He forecasts an average gross of two thousand dollars per week in the growing season. There is a compelling simplicity in his concept (although the full realization will take enormous skill and stamina). In the early 1990s Davis estimated that sales of specialty vegetables in greater Chicago exceeded $20 million, $12 million for the wholesale restaurant market and $8 million for retail sale. Cabrini Greens could sell unique specialty crops that command prices of five to seven dollars per pound to two main customers: three-star or higher restaurants, and the twenty-five local retail farmers' markets. "We grow eight blocks away from our buyers. Who else can guarantee same-day-harvested young vegetables and salad greens?" In the long term, they could add on a mail-order business offering salad dressings, flavored vinegars, herbal teas, certain specialty crop and plant seedlings, and catnip products. "There are two hundred and fifty varieties of potatoes and three thousand varieties of beans. We could grow specialty and heirloom varieties that no one else grows for our customers," said Davis, who has received donated seeds from Seed Savers Exchange and Burpee. Already he has lined up twelve restaurant customers, and is focusing presently on growing for a small number of them, including Charlie Trotter's and Michael Jordan's. As for the farmer's markets, children and adults could staff it on Saturdays. Products could include prewashed salad greens, packaged in resealable bags in quantities convenient for working people to bring for lunch. Cut flowers, specialty vegetables, and herbs could be sold in bulk.

The business plan includes three long-term key objectives. First, an organizational infrastructure must be built so that the community can own the project. Second, the business must grow so that it can pay for itself, the main expense being salaries for the kids and their adult supervisors. Third, an educational component, which links the market garden with the schools, where the gardeners can learn math, science, and business skills, must be developed.

Currently each of these goals is in an embryonic stage. Dan Underwood has been hired as day-to-day supervisor, but more volunteer (and eventually paid) adults are needed to help with supervision. The kids are being paid for the hours they put in (about $250 per child for the season), and they also receive a share in the income from the sale of produce; but to expand beyond the present program size (nine girls and six boys), more acreage will have to be cultivated. This year Dan Underwood developed a year-round program of speakers and hands-on projects for a class of seventh graders at the Schiller School. Twelve chefs from local upscale restaurants were invited to prepare dishes with the class—a pair of students working with each chef—and finish with a food tasting. (That's when the kids first tasted purple potato salad.) Two girls asked their chef for a job in her restaurant. "If you stay with Cabrini Greens until you are sixteen, you've got a job," she promised. The Wizard, a black artist who paints gardens, exhibited his work to the seventh graders and talked to them about the medicinal and nutritional wild plants found around Cabrini-Green, such as dandelions, wild carrots, and narrow-leaf plaintain. His real name is Cush, but he's called "The Wizard" because of his knowledge of the medicinal uses of plants.

In early spring 1994, the students planted seeds in trays and started them under grow lights for the Cabrini Greens gardens. From the class of twenty-five seventh graders, Dan selected many of the gardeners working with him this summer, his criteria being the students' interest as well as their parents' interest and commitment. He hopes to expand the classes to include all the seventh- and eighth-graders, about one hundred students, and to focus in class on drying, packaging, and making value-added products from their garden produce such as salsas and sauces.

The practical skills the kids can learn in connection with the garden project are boundless. Davis talks about computer programs that simulate a garden plot, a mechanics class where kids learn to repair rototillers, business math oriented around costing out a market garden and learning how to do a balance sheet, and teaching plant propagation in science class. Underwood wants to keep the kids all the way through high school and help them get into college. "Not, okay you're in this program for two years and then you're on your own." He also wants them to see that they can run a business, that "they don't have to sell drugs to make money." Right now he could use a few sixteen-to-eighteen-year-olds to put up fences, hook up water lines, and use the heavy equipment independently. Like Jack, he wants these kids to learn how to work (even while he wants a lot more for them, like camping trips to Lake Owasippee). "A lot of people don't know how to work, they have never learned how to work."

What are the obstacles to Cabrini Greens' success? "People don't think it can work," answered Jack, referring to some who have written off inner-city people as unwilling to work. And "we need capital for equipment and Dan's salary." The income from the vegetables pays the kids, but doesn't cover the cost of tools or a rototiller. When Davis solicited start-up capital some business people criticized him for trying to subsidize the project, but he retorts that commercial agriculture is subsidized to the teeth, beginning with water rates in California. Some foundations and nonprofit audiences have found their mission and philosophy too market-oriented, said Charlie Kubert, a volunteer grant writer and gardener for Cabrini Greens. Both Davis and Kubert agree that they may need ten, twenty, or thirty acres to fund all the salaries. It's nearly impossible to get a reliable supply of produce from two-and-a-half acres, especially when they are separated into five individual gardens on different CHA properties. "CHA gives lip service to the project," Kubert added, "because it helps their image. But they don't come through with fencing and long-term security for the gardens."

There are several market obstacles as well. For one, consumers are accustomed to eating anything they want at any time of year, and most are not committed to buying locally-grown, seasonal produce. A potential customer, like nearby Whole Foods, a supermarket and restaurant complex that features organic and wholesome food products, prefers to buy from the same supplier twelve months of the year. (Jack and Dan hold their business meetings in the Whole Foods restaurant, where they eye purple potatoes retailing for $1.69 a

*The purple
potato patch at
Cabrini-Green.*

pound, yellow peppers for $3.99 a pound, and baby French beans for $6.99 a pound—all vegetables that Cabrini Greens grows and could supply seasonally to the store.) For this reason, Davis has targeted local restaurants, which are more flexible in buying, as a better market. He illustrates this point with the story of how he found watercress growing wild in a section of one garden where a broken water pipe had created a small wet area. They harvested the watercress and sold it to Charlie Trotter's restaurant for five dollars a pound.

Is Davis in this for good? "I'd like to be," he said, "but there are people who could help." Foundations and corporations could make a substantive financial commitment for start-up capital. Seed companies have made donations, but Cabrini Greens could use larger investment from the public, nonprofit, and private sectors. And the CHA could follow through with repairing and maintaining fencing so Cabrini Greens could focus its energies on the gardens.

The Not-for-Profit Side

I want to be a blessing with these gardens and then I will be blessed.
—Louis Berkhalter, Gardener, Flannery Apartments for Seniors

Dan Underwood returned from a week of camping in mid-July with the Explorer scouts, and weeds were everywhere. In just one hot, humid, and rainy week in Chicago, they had spread throughout the two large plots of lettuce and blue potatoes, the newly started gardens at Division and Larrabee Streets at Cabrini-Green, and the fifteen hundred tomato plants at the seniors' housing facility at 3030 West 21st Street on the West Side. Worse, someone had pulled up a few dozen wire cages that bound the most mature tomato plants. Despite these setbacks, Dan will not give up the annual midsummer camping trip, as Jack Davis would like, now that he is garden supervisor.

No farmer would dream of leaving the farm for a week in July, said Davis. But Underwood feels that although the kids need the gardens in the city, they also need to go on "star hikes," to forage for edible foods, to go canoeing and camping in the woods; kids need nature both in the city and in the country. Jack Davis knows that Dan Underwood's participation is vital to the future of Cabrini Greens: "He *fits*, but he's as market-minded as a social worker." Davis wants to concentrate on teaching kids to grow market products, and to leave the other life skills they need to learn to parents, teachers, and social workers.

FACING PAGE:
*The Flannery
Apartments
and gardens.*

The differences between the businessman and the social worker extend to the contrary positions they have taken on the garden at Thomas Flannery Apartments for Senior Citizens, 252 units of CHA housing close to Cabrini-Green. Here resident seniors grow every vegetable one can find in the produce section of a well-stocked supermarket, as well as fruit and flowers, in this large, lush, beautifully staked and organized communal garden. The land had originally been plowed and planted two years previously by Jack Davis and the kids from Cabrini-Green, and was gardened again by Cabrini Greens the following year. Jack pronounced this to be the best soil of all the land they farm in the city; he found the opportunistic watercress here. The long-term business plan for the Flannery garden was that seniors would supervise the children in planting, weeding, and harvesting, and that both groups would be paid an hourly or weekly wage.

A takeover happened this year: Presley Robinson, Jr., who had a plot in the Cabrini Greens garden at Flannery, emerged as the leader of the gardening seniors, and talked with other gardeners there about having the garden "for and by seniors." They brought the issue up for a vote to the Flannery tenants' council, won the vote, and "took over the garden." They have divided the garden into two rectangular plots, each one dedicated to one of the twin high-rise apartment buildings at Flannery. Three "master gardeners" maintain large plots in which they grow food for many resident seniors who cannot garden; nine others are assisted by the three master gardeners with small plots they have been given within the two large rectangular garden areas.

One assisted gardener, Mary Dingle, asked wryly, "How do you have a garden when you can't bend over?" She pointed her cane toward master gardener Louis Berkhalter. "That's how. He dug it up, set it out, waters it, limes it—all at his own expense." Berkhalter had a hand in all the gardens on his side, as well as his own bountiful plot. "I think he looks at plants and they grow." Mary added that she does the same with houseplants. "I got a forest in there and Louis got a forest out here." She had enlisted her neighbor Charles Brown to collect and carry some cucumbers, okra, tomatoes, and white potatoes from

her plot, and talked about plans for making "cha-cha" and fried green tomatoes. "Brown, take two cucumbers for yourself," she good-naturedly ordered him.

The umbrageous "forest" in Mary Dingle's apartment creates a canopy over the collectibles of a lifetime. "My thing is my plants, my stuffed animals [which own the sofa], my photos [which cover the walls], and *sometimes my grandkids*." She described how her daughter will give her a dying plant, and how she then plays music for it ("people think I'm crazy"), pets it, loves it, talks to it, and "it just blooms."

Louis Berkhalter spends three seasons "growing for the building." He raises turnips and turnip greens all year-round except December and January. In February he gets turnip and mustard greens going. Elderly shut-ins tell him what they want and he grows it. They look down upon his generous and varied garden from their apartments and find their favorites: okra, yellow squash,

140

purple-top turnips, horseradish, watermelon, swiss chard, string beans, shell peas, canteloupes, red onions, corn, buttercup squash, and mustard greens.

Louis left his home in Mississippi at eighteen, joined the army, and was stationed in Germany and eventually sent to Vietnam. After the war, he worked in a machine shop in Chicago. Disabled by a car accident, he is younger at age fifty-three than most residents at Flannery. He plans, when his pension starts in 1996, to go back to Mississippi and buy equipment to farm land he owns there. "Can't nothin' beat gardening. I meditate when I'm doing it. I grew up farming and gardening. This is it; this is my life."

An uncommonly calm and present man, Louis was momentarily shaken; an insect resembling a cucumber beetle had infested his corn plants. For the first time, he resorted to dusting with Sevin, a pesticide; otherwise all the master gardeners in the Flannery garden only sprinkle lime around plants to deter insects, explaining that it is a tradition that goes back to their family farms in Arkansas and Mississippi. Ladybugs alighted on plants everywhere in the garden, a sign of its health and, with this one exception, pesticide-free horticulture.

Louis described making a garden as "redoing a family," where you take care of plants like you do a baby. "You gotta love it. If you don't love, it won't grow. We have a lot of kids like that—not loved." The subject moves quickly from plants to politics. "We need more leaders, *not politicians*, more Martin Luther Kings." Everybody needs them, he insisted, white people and black people; not football players and basketball players, but leaders. "Like that guy in Chicago, Judge Eugene Pinkston. Came in with a new party, stood for everybody, not just blacks. Ran for mayor in the Rainbow Coalition."

Getting back to the seniors for whom he grows, Louis described their faces when someone brings them out to the garden. "My garden *el-e-vies* . . ." He draws it out to make his point. ". . . You know, lifts them up." Until he had done the garden, he had only met a few people living in Flannery. "Now, people watch from their windows, they know me for this garden." Tall and strong despite the car accident, Berkhalter is a fully spiritual man for whom the garden is a place of prayer and meditation and even grace. "The Bible says, 'I will make you a blessing to all the countries and then I will bless you.' I want to be a blessing with these gardens and then I will be blessed."

Elizabeth Robinson, another of the three gardeners-in-charge, and president of the Flannery Garden Association, keeps her garden going all year-round. A new row of purple-top turnip seeds had just germinated, Kentucky

FACING PAGE:
Louis Berkhalter's garden.

Wonder pole beans climbed supports, and another variety of bean grew up a frame she salvaged from the trash. She grows everything Louis does, plus scarlet basil, sweet peppers, head lettuce, and rutabagas, with flowers intermixed—zinnias, marigolds, ageratum, something she named "princess flower," and the lanceolate leaves of gladioluses. Robinson explained that she belongs to a garden club in Grand Rapids, Michigan, and that they sent her the gladiolus bulbs as a bonus when she ordered her seeds.

She pointed to collards and cabbage: "This is for the community. We just want to call this a backyard garden for the seniors." But there are rules. People can't just come in the garden; they have to ask for the vegetables, and Elizabeth collects them. Robinson works from 6:30 until about 10:30 or 11:00 each morning, "until it gets too warm," and sometimes "if I feel like it, I come out at five." People watch her work from their apartments, like the 108-year-old woman who looks for Robinson and asks about her if she doesn't see her.

The reticent, soft-spoken gardener let the luxuriant garden speak for itself, only disclosing her skill and feeling for horticulture when pressed with questions. She pointed to the uncultivatable wet area which abuts her garden—the

Elizabeth Robinson in her garden.

Chicago

spot where Jack Davis had harvested watercress last year—saying that she would like to expand there. "I wouldn't leave anything unturned." As a child, she worked with her father on his farm in Arkansas. They grew everything she plants here, plus cotton, and never used any pesticide or fertilizer, only lime. She recalled how her father would plant turnip seeds in with the cotton seeds, and cupped her hands to show how huge the turnip "bottoms" grew—six inches across! "This is very good soil, very mellow."

Presley Robinson, Jr. (who is no relation to Elizabeth Robinson), is soft- and slow-spoken, like Elizabeth, and is religious like Louis; but his words can cut like a surgical knife. The idea of taking the garden from Jack Davis and Cabrini Greens and making it one "by and for seniors" came to him when he was "sittin' under a tree meditatin'." He loves growing flowers within the thick rows of crowder peas, black-eyed peas, carrots, snow peas, hot peppers, sweet potatoes, muskmelons ("they do smell loud") and watermelon, although he doesn't know or need to know the flowers' names. His favorite part of his garden is the sequence of marigolds, coleus, and salvia (whose names he doesn't know) that he planted and spaced to spell the word LOVE. Presley meditates in his garden: "It's where I get my peace. I love to see things grow. If we as human beings could only grow in a positive state of consciousness like these plants."

Presley's political temperament came forth when he talked about the garden takeover. "I'm still waitin' on my forty acres and a mule," he gestured toward the half-acre garden as a piece of a long-overdue promise. He recalled growing up playing with a white boy in Arkansas, and how, when the friend turned twelve, the boy's father told Presley to call his son "Mr." Presley fought in Germany and France during the second world war and gained "experience" there. "We fought the same war. When it came to eatin' and sleepin', 'whites over here, blacks over there.' But on the battlefield, every man grabbed a hole where he could get one!" After the war, he did "everything" in Chicago: swept floors, washed dishes, did laundry, worked in the steel mills and in aircraft manufacturing, and took up body and fender work and welding in vocational school. "I've been through the flood of life here on Earth."

An animus festers between Presley Robinson, Jr., and Jack Davis. Presley says that Jack is racist; Jack says that Presley doesn't like white people. Presley retorts that when he looks at a person, he doesn't see color. "I'm a universal and I go by God's law." Jack says that *he* first plowed and started up the garden, that he and Dan are always looking for land, that the soil at Flannery is the best soil

*Presley
Robinson, Jr.
in his garden.*

of all the market gardens, and that he's willing to give the seniors some space.
Presley says "the soil looks good but looks are deceiving. It's nothin' but clay, and
the black in it come from the [decomposed] grass." Jack says that Presley stole
the kids' t-shirts and hats that he recently stored at Flannery. Presley says that
Jack never paid him when he worked with kids in the Flannery garden last year.

Dan Underwood says that they should let the seniors keep the garden. The
seniors at Flannery have their plots staked out as soon as the snow melts. They
are the best gardeners, keeping a constant, vigilant eye on the garden. As Dan
sees it, Cabrini Greens got the seniors' garden going by rototilling the land, but
now the seniors can take care of it themselves. They could even sell vegetables
to other seniors in the building. "Presley is the self-appointed chief and competitive with Jack. Jack is disappointed that the seniors don't want Cabrini Greens
back. But I told Jack, 'This is good that they want to take care of it themselves.'"
As Davis the businessman sees it, Cabrini Greens cannot afford to lose its capital
investment to hostile takeovers. As Underwood the social worker sees it, the

gardens at Flannery—now tended and managed by the residents—are a success story in community ownership.

A Source for Lessons

The common goal shared by Jack Davis and Dan Underwood is a counterpoint to the animosity between Jack and Presley. "Jack and I agreed on a five-year plan," said Dan. "In five years, we'll have twenty acres and four hundred kids." Their different competencies, even their differing world views, are a strength thus far in this project. Each brings what the other needs to make a concept— so linear from the market side, so circuitous from the social side—work.

Gardens in public housing projects are not entirely new; but the entrepreneurial effort of Cabrini Greens, with its emphasis on job training for ten-to-fifteen-year-olds, is novel. In the late 1950s the Chicago Housing Authority initiated a program that housing authorities in other major cities looked to with promise: the establishment of tenant gardens for grounds beautification. The high-rise public housing built in the 1950s had abundant open space: The buildings covered only about 15 to 20 percent of a housing site. The buildings were so densely populated—Robert Taylor Homes in Chicago, with fifteen thousand people, was the largest of the city's public housing projects, and Cabrini-Green had close to ten thousand residents—that the projects were like neighborhoods unto themselves, except that they the lacked necessary ingredients for an urban neighborhood to work, elements such as diversity of income and commercial activity; well-managed buildings; safe, busy streets; and public space. Even today there are no large supermarkets, no banks, and no clothing stores in the Cabrini-Green neighborhood, only the typical commerce of the ghetto: a convenience store, numerous liquor stores, and storefronts with signs that declare CHECKS CASHED.

The CHA beautification concept engaged tenants to work with maintenance staff on selecting garden sites, and in planning, planting, and maintaining flower gardens. The Authority sponsored an annual contest for "the most beautiful housing project in Chicago," and the citywide janitors' union awarded cash prizes to maintenance men in the project with the most beautiful flower beds. In its day, the program was hailed as an innovation, and other housing authorities in major cities like New York and Philadelphia, as well as Norfolk, Seattle, and Gary, adapted the idea. In some cases, they were solely tenant-run; in others, partnerships with elite garden clubs developed. Generally an annual contest for the best gardens imbued the concept with good-spirited, competitive energy.

A tenant of today's Chicago public housing could scarcely imagine that anything beautiful ever grew on the vast, gray, barren space around Henry Horner Homes, Rockwell Gardens, or Cabrini-Green. Mounds of dirt with a few clumps of annuals were perched at several corners of Cabrini-Green—added like an afterthought in late July, 1994. Otherwise this landscape, except for the Cabrini Greens gardens, is as Jane Jacobs forecast it would become: "generous expanses of shunned areas," grounds destined to be "deserted parks." With mordant wit, Jacobs assailed the vast aprons of vacant land around high-rise public housing that were considered a middle-class amenity by urban planners of the day: "If all controls were lifted from housing-project malls, and these dead underused lots found their natural economic level, junk yards and used-car lots are exactly what would sprout in many of them."

The surprise of Cabrini Greens is precisely that a tractor and a bunch of kids planting some specialty crops has turned Jacobs' almost sibylline commentary on its head. A half-acre of mixed salad greens and a quarter-acre of purple potatoes fills and greens the erstwhile empty, gray land within view of four high-rises and the Schiller School on Scott Street. Off Division Street, in another section of Cabrini-Green, Dan Underwood had the long mall-like stretches of unused land plowed, and the kids planted potatoes, peppers, basil, and squash. A teacher in a nearby daycare center has asked to use one of the plots for her pre-schoolers.

The vegetable gardens aren't as pretty and well-weeded as the early CHA beautification gardens must have been; they are serious produce gardens. "We're organic," explains Jack Davis. "I'm not into beautiful gardens. We've got weeds." But the quality of the produce and the acuity that guides the market plan—the willingness, for example, to grow unique varieties of potatoes, to garden organically, and to target the market of three-star and higher restaurants—make this project almost one of a kind. There are no models to imitate, only a handful of other financially struggling entrepreneurial community garden ventures with which to exchange some lessons learned.

Recently the Urban Resources Initiative at Yale University's School of Forestry and Environmental Studies evaluated five urban gardening programs that included a revenue-generating component, all in low-income, inner-city neighborhoods. Some worked with drug treatment program participants, others with

Day care plot across from Cabrini-Green.

inner-city children and teenagers; one was neighborhood-based, and another was Cathrine Sneed's Garden Project in San Francisco for people leaving jail. The entrepreneurial activities included opening a farmer's market; selling firewood, compost, herbs, herbed vinegars, flowers, and a range of homegrown produce at farmers' markets; and operating year-round commercial solar greenhouses. The range of start-up costs, often supplied by government grants and supplemented by foundation monies, was fifteen thousand to three hundred thousand dollars. The study found that none of the projects was producing a profit, and only one—the passive solar greenhouse project, which is older than the other projects by about ten years and is operated by a resident-initiated, neighborhood coalition—generated sales that contributed substantially to its operating budget. All of the projects were more successful in meeting their social and educational goals—teaching horticulture and marketing skills to low-income youth, teaching life skills to drug-addicted people and those released from jail—than their market goals. If Jack Davis can capitalize Cabrini Greens and make it pay for itself, which is his goal, he will have rare and valuable lessons to offer sister projects in Chicago and in other inner cities.

Hundreds of public, nonprofit, private, and community-based groups are working to restore Chicago to its motto, *urbs in horto,* or "city in a garden." In the early 1900s landscape architect Jens Jensen helped design Chicago's extensive municipal park system, and pioneered prairie landscapes and urban children's gardens. CitySpace, an ambitious joint effort of the City of Chicago, the Chicago Park District, and the Forest Preserve district of Cook County, is inventorying Chicago's existing and potential open space—including the municipal parks, schoolyards, abandoned railroad corridors, and the city's estimated fifty-six thousand vacant lots—in order to create an overall plan for more open and green space in the city. ChicagoRivers has been hailed as the most comprehensive urban river planning effort in the country. Federal, municipal, and county agencies vested in some part of the river have coalesced with Friends of the Chicago River to study the river quality, develop long-term management needs, and identify demonstration projects that make a difference on a single reach of the river, even at the neighborhood level. Other projects include Mayor Richard Daley's *Urbs in Horto/*Tree Fund, which plants more than ten thousand trees annually. The mayor was born on Arbor Day and is, in his own words, "tree crazy." The Openlands Project has a goal of establishing one thousand miles of linear greenways through and around the city. Chicago has been picked as one of four cities to pilot a federal program, here called the Urban Resource Partnership for Chicago, intended to build community-based efforts for addressing environmental issues such as natural habitats, water quality, open space, and environmental education.

Cabrini Greens, at two-and-one-half acres of market gardens on "gray and shunned" public housing land, and even at its five-year goal of twenty acres and four hundred kids, is modest in scale compared to Openlands, CityScape, the *Urbs in Horto/*Tree Fund, and ChicagoRivers. But Cabrini Greens is attempting something more ambitious in scope: to teach horticulture, business skills, and self-respect to children from some of Chicago's most embattled public housing and public schools; and to make the program self-financing. In so doing, it is reclaiming castaway yet organically rich urban land for productive and harmonious uses, while imagining a future for children otherwise foreclosed on by every societal and public institution.

Why So Many Women?

PREVIOUS PAGE:
*Lorraine Harris,
Peggy Williams,
and a friend in
the Enchanted
Marston Gardens
in Philadelphia.*

WALKING INTO THE ANNUAL SUNDAY BRUNCH FOR PHILADELPHIA GREEN community gardeners in March 1995, I was reminded anew how active and powerful women are in the community garden movement. Of the many hundreds gathered on this final, festive day of the Philadelphia Flower Show to celebrate the gardens, most were women of color from the city's neighborhoods. Is there a larger, broader history of women and gardens, I have pondered throughout the writing of this book, which underlies the community garden movement? What meaning—personal, social, and political—have gardens held for women of different classes and ethnicities? Have rural women loved and kept gardens like the urban women I encountered?

A Saving Love

In the 1950s Eudora Welty introduced her friend and fellow writer Elizabeth Lawrence to the southern market bulletins where farmers would place classified ads for farm goods, and gardeners advertised perennials and herbs. The market bulletins offered a glimpse of rural life in the Deep South: Their classified ads included homeless families seeking lodging and jobs picking cotton; a widow advertising for a companion in exchange for room and board; puppies in need of a home; listings for mules, cordwood, and bales of alfalfa hay for sale by farmers, and garden plants for sale by farm women.

Welty placed Lawrence's name on the mailing list for the *Mississippi Market Bulletin*, and this professional garden writer initiated an exchange of letters and plants with southern rural women that lasted from the late 1950s to the mid-1970s. Lawrence's book *Gardening for Love* was named for the hundreds of "hard-working farm women who are never too tired, when their farm work is done, to cultivate their flower gardens." They found time to collect seeds, separate and dig plants, and pack them for mailing to sister gardeners known only through the mail. Lawrence found to her immense pleasure that these farm women were reliable letter writers, if one included a self-addressed envelope and stamp with a request for seeds, bulbs, or plants. They answered her questions about plant care "freely, willingly, and with love." Lawrence delighted in the "sweet country names" that survived thanks to these women: names like candlestick lilies, white star jessamine, prince's feather, fluffy-ruffles fern, and lady's eardrop. Many reached back, Lawrence reckoned, to Shakespeare and the Bible.

Lawrence dubbed "these old ladies—and an occasional gentleman—who sell flowers through the mail . . . amateurs in the true sense of the word: they garden for love." She designated their love a "saving love" because, as Native American farmers of the Southwest and Mexico still do in their kitchen and market gardens, rural women cultivated many plants that would otherwise be lost in the homogenization of commercial seed production for surburban gardens. Only in the dooryard gardens of these amateurs, in remote farm yards and around farm houses, could certain plants still be found.

In her history of women and plants, Jennifer Bennett describes the horticulturally rich world of medieval and Renaissance village women, the foresisters of these southern farm women. Not likely to travel beyond the nearest town in their lifetimes, they created a complex world of plants from which they produced many household and village necessities using the entire plant—root, leaf, and flower. The homeopathic properties of their plants, as well as their fragrances and unique qualities, were as well-known to some women, says Bennett, as the characteristics of their own families and friends.

The inventors of agriculture were primarily women of the New Stone Age. Creation, the renewal of seasons, and eventually agriculture were attributed to goddesses called Maia, Pachamama, Ninlil, Demeter, and Ceres, who were ritually invoked for good harvests. Women selected the best plants, and saved seeds from the most pest- and drought-resistant, the largest and fastest maturing. Over centuries, these farmers and plant breeders brought the original wild species of crops like tomatoes and maize much closer to their modern, domesticated varieties. Likewise, the majority of community gardeners in inner cities are women, women of color whose historical relationships to plants extend back to the agrarian South, as well as farther back to Africa, islands in the Caribbean, and to Latin American and Asian countries, where traditions of subsistence gardens link them to the very origins of intentional agriculture.

In the centuries between the beginning of agriculture some ten thousand years ago and the Greening of Harlem, the practice of gardening has been stratified by wealth and by gender. In mid-sixteenth century Germany, for example, five different genres of gardens and parks could be found, much as we have today. Ordinary gardens for the household were planted with vegetables, vines, and small orchards. Medicinal gardens contained various healing herbs, which constituted the basic household pharmacopoeia. Ornamental gardens mixed utilitarian plants with plants selected for admiration and adornment. More elegant gardens were planted solely to enhance an estate or monastery, such as sitting and strolling gardens containing arbors, gazebos, and curving pathways, and whose plantings included prized species of trees. Surpassing them all in scale and prominence were show gardens and parks, appointed with splendid waterworks, ponds, and buildings, and outfitted with squares for tournaments, all built by wealthy men, princes, or the state. One might envision these varieties of gardens as a pyramid, whose generous base comprises the millions of subsistence, kitchen, and medicinal gardens planted and tended by women, and which were central to household economy, village health, and local biodiversity. The pyramid's apex is the discrete number of palatial show parks and gardens, commissioned by aristocratic aesthetes, princes, and nobles, and designed by men who had the societal standing of artists and poets, which functioned as public monuments attesting to their wealth and power.

For countless centuries women have toiled in gardens for survival, for relief from house and field work, and in keeping with or in rebellion against the cult of floral femininity. Men of means, for their part, built private horticultural estates as symbols of wealth; founded horticultural societies that excluded women (even though botany was deemed a suitable, not overly taxing science for women, and half the botanists of early nineteenth-century New England were women); designed and sited monumental parks in cities as a respite from their environment-degrading industries; and sought wildernesses against which to test themselves.

The garden was both a village midwife's pharmacy and a homesick pioneer woman's solace in an alien world. The garden was often the primary source of intellectual stimulation for the eighteenth- and nineteenth-century woman botanist who had neither the financial nor social support that her brother could have commanded to travel widely for specimens. And it was frequently the most accessible spot of nature and source of beauty for the urban and rural poor who might never travel beyond their neighborhoods.

The contemporary writer Alice Walker has asked how a black woman of her grandmothers' day could have become an artist. "How was the creativity of the black woman kept alive . . . when for most of the years black people have been in America, it was a punishable crime for a black person to read or write?" Examining her own mother's work-burdened life in the post-Reconstruction South, Walker found an answer: The garden was a space and time apart in which the artist could arise.

The garden itself was an artistic medium, like the church choir, that a black woman could use without harassment or retribution. Her materials—seeds and plants; soil, kitchen compost, and manure; a picket fence or stones for a border—were affordable, or procured by bartering with a neighbor, or simply free. Walker's mother had "ambitious" flower gardens with no fewer than fifty different varieties, which bloomed from March until November. She watered her flowers and prepared new beds before going to the fields; she divided and replanted perennials and bulbs and pruned her bushes when she returned from the fields and then after supper until dark descended. People came from across three counties to witness her artistry; friends and neighbors received cuttings from the gardens' largesse. In her garden (and only there) Walker's mother was radiant, "ordering the universe in the image of her personal conception of Beauty." This informal artist's gardens were the quotidian example of art for her daughter, and they constituted a "screen of blooms" that eased the family's rural southern poverty. Had Walker's mother, like Rachel Bagby and so many African-American community gardeners, emigrated north with her family to work in the factories of Chicago or North Philadelphia, she might have become a master gardener at Flannery Apartments for Senior Citizens, or joined the Heritage Eight to pass on to city children the horticultural knowledge of the southern African-American.

Gardens were a lifeline for farm women who might not meet another woman throughout the week except at church on Sundays. The garden was a wall-less "room of one's own" for poor black women confined to shacks and monotonous work in someone else's fields. And amid the chaos and nihilism of war, gardens have saved gardeners from despair.

In 1947 Clare Leighton addressed a national meeting of women horticulturalists in St. Paul, Minnesota. She, too, declared herself an amateur gardener, "a lover of working in the earth." Never, she said, had the world been more in need of gardens to remind by their presence that some life is beyond destruction. "While Hitler's armies overrode Europe, even while the armies trod down the grass, there were forces beyond those powers of destruction. There were the same forces that still went out and made the trees bud, and leaves come out." She told of a country woman in England who wrote her to describe how she tended her garden, planting bulbs and collecting seeds from her annuals, after cleaning up from the bombs and finishing her war work. "I realize," the woman wrote, "that it is only in this that I seem to have enough hope to go on living."

The war had ended; so why, Leighton asked her audience, were gardens so necessary today? The bombs have ceased, she replied to her own question, but the war has left a dispirited world, one filled with anxiety and without "a long-distance view of life." Working in the earth, cultivating its life, restores "a sense of basic spiritual security on life." Whether it is an old tin can on a tenement windowsill holding a bit of soil in which a handful of seeds have been planted, or acres of elegant gardens, what matters is that *the garden gives back*. They make us yearn for the first shoots of spring and enable us to stretch summer into fall with cool-tolerant plants. They attune and attach us to weather: We scan the sky for rain in dry seasons and sun in wet periods. And the garden year is marked by rituals: maple sap flowing, strawberries ripe for picking, the first corn of the season, new potatoes, autumn harvest, and even the first hard frost. Leighton concluded with a parable about a dandelion growing through rubble in the Bethlehem-Fairfield naval shipyard near Baltimore. As she watched one of its seeds waft across a naval destroyer, she reflected that the seed held more power than the ship. Left to itself, the steel ship would rust and decay. "But that one tiny dandelion seed had in itself the force of immortality beyond my lifetime, because it held inside that tiny little shell the power of growth."

The Uncounted Wealth of Gardens

At the neighborhood and household level, where women dwell and work on the surrounding land, they identify, collect, cultivate, and conserve large numbers of plant and animal species. Yet the value of this work, like that of community gardening, is generally not counted in the economy because such work is unpaid and not market-based; nor is it recorded in environmental history because it is considered the minor, insignificant work of many "ordinary" women and not the major, heroic drama of the rare Great Man; nor has this work been documented, until recently, by the mainstream media because the billions of examples of the "homely act of earthkeeping," as poet Robin Morgan calls her gardening, are neither *grand* nor *romantic*.

There is nothing romantic about being dispossessed of land while you feed the majority of the world. According to United Nations statistics, women hold title to one percent of the world's land while they produce more than 50 percent of the world's food. In sub-Saharan Africa women produce more than 80 percent of the food, and in Asia between 50 and 60 percent. Rural families throughout the world eat from women's gardens. But labor statistics, as political economist Marilyn Waring documents, most often measure wage labor, not subsistence work; so women's contribution through gardening to the world's food supply is chronically underestimated. While the grand parks, public gardens, and agribusinesses of the world reflect the patrimony of our imperial and industrial eras, it is very likely that the wealth of biodiversity preserved by humans resides largely in the dooryard gardens and the communal forests of anonymous women gardeners and agroforesters.

The Global Garden

The gap between the rich and poor in the United States is widening, a phenomenon of the last decade which has no counterpart in any other wealthy democracy. Moreover, the proportion of young people finishing high school dropped from the late 1960s to the late 1980s. Economically, our inner cities have more in common with faltering third world countries that are indentured to foreign aid and can no longer feed themselves, than they do to their adjacent suburbs. Parts of many United States cities are barely distinguishable from the poorest third world cities.

At first glance, community gardens may seem an unlikely and unremarkable means of urban renewal. An anachronism? A naive throwback to pre-industrial times? Cathrine Sneed had wondered, even as she proposed the Horticulture Project to Sheriff Michael Hennessey in the early 1980s, whether anyone would respect working in soil. *Hadn't farming lost its dignity to the briefcase?* In fact, the urban community garden, with its potential for feeding households and generating local cottage industry, with its power to restore a measure of community life, and with its capacity to recycle organic wastes, is thriving throughout the world: in Karachi, La Paz, Hong Kong, Nairobi, Dakar, Dar es Salaam, and Bangkok, as well as in Philadelphia, Detroit, Newark, and Los Angeles. Globally, about two hundred million urban dwellers are urban farmers. Most of these farmers are women, and they provide food and income for about seven hundred million people. Is it so surprising that urban women of color would use community gardens to repair the fabric of our inner cities? Neither nostalgic for a pastoral past, nor Luddite in its sensibility, the inner-city community garden movement restores a nature banished from the industrial city, and offers a degree of self-sufficiency and neighborhood security, achievements that elude the master plans of urban planning experts.

Indeed, the key to self-determination that so many have found in millions of market gardens, woodlots, and greening projects, also opens broad paths of friendship and exchange between global gardeners. In 1991 Wangari Maathai flew from her home in Kenya to San Francisco, where she received the Goldman Environmental Prize for her work in creating the Green Belt Movement. Fourteen years earlier Dr. Maathai, Kenya's first woman Ph.D., had planted seven trees in her backyard and initiated a movement to stem desertification, a movement that has developed into Africa's leading environmental organization. By the early 1990s, ten million trees had been planted in six African countries, and fifty thousand African women are employed working in fifteen hundred tree nurseries. The Green Belt Movement is both an environmental and a human rights movement, Maathai explains, because as poor women learn to care for tree seedlings, they earn income, learn about nutrition and discuss family planning, and gain self-esteem. Before leaving the Bay Area, Wangari Maathai visited Cathrine Sneed and the Horticulture Project at the county jail in San Bruno. Each is the other's hero. Speaking of her respect for Maathai, Cathrine Sneed also captured the saving power of gardens across time and continents that Rachel Bagby, Iris Brown, Bernadette Cozart, Dan Underwood, and Sister Maureen O'Hara have known: "We are doing the same thing. We are using a garden to empower people. She reminds me that this is not just a San Francisco thing. The earth can transform people while they are helping the environment." After touring the eight acres of vegetables, herbs, and flowers that student inmates had grown in raised beds and were harvesting for San Francisco soup kitchens, Maathai told the small audience of students and visitors: "We came from the earth and we will go back to the earth, but between those two destinies we must care for ourselves and reach out to others."

EPILOGUE

THE LANDSCAPE OF COMMUNITY GARDENS IN OUR CITIES HAS CHANGED SINCE I began researching this book three years ago, and the changes are mainly salutary. For one, the community garden movement is growing in breadth. Projects like the Greening of Harlem have caught the imagination of public media and funders alike, and are expanding substantively. The Greening of Harlem now has thirty gardens, one of which is a vineyard being planned with an Oregon vintner who contacted Bernadette Cozart after he heard her interviewed on National Public Radio. The Garden Project in San Francisco has become a nationally-recognized model for crime prevention, and the Tree Corps employs more than twenty people full-time. The School Garden Corps, a new enterprise of the Garden Project, helps young welfare mothers gain skills and employment as they create and maintain organic gardens at ten elementary schools where their children attend class.

The gardens are diversifying. In late 1994 *The New York Times* carried a story about the resurgence of restorative gardens in hospices, nursing homes, and treatment centers. Gardens for the sick, which were often the primary context for healing in monasteries and convents of the Middle Ages, disappeared with the rise of Western medicine. They are now reappearing where medicine has no immediate cure and offers little solace, for example at the AIDS unit in Terence Cardinal Cook Health Center in East Harlem, in St. Michael Rehabilitation Center outside of Texarkana, and at the Marin County General Hospital Cancer Center, among others.

Something else, we might call it building institutional capacity or depth, is in the works. Nonprofit community greening organizations are initiating a new generation of skills-building in community gardeners to ensure that the gardens become the richest possible social and environmental asset to their neighborhoods. For example, the four major nonprofit garden organizations of Boston have formed a new collaborative called Garden Futures to assess the capital and maintenance needs, as well as funding, leadership, and educational needs, of the fifty garden projects and three thousand households with which they work. The goal of the collaborative is to create a permanent capital and operations fund for the gardens, and to develop leadership and horticultural training for gardeners, on topics that range from composting to conflict resolution, over a two- to three-year period. Garden Futures is being supported financially by many local and regional foundations and is linked to the city of Boston's environmental programs.

In a sister venture, the American Community Gardening Association (ACGA) recently established a two-year program called "From the Roots Up: Training Community Greeners." Supported by the Merck Family Fund, this program will give comprehensive training to approximately ten emerging city-wide greening organizations serving low- to moderate-income communities. The specific goals of this project are to assist new community garden and greening programs with institutional issues such as board development and fund raising, as well as more specific neighborhood-focused skills in community organizing, food production, economic opportunities, and intergenerational projects.

The ACGA estimates that municipal governments and nonprofit organizations supported by private philanthropy operate gardening programs in about two hundred and fifty cities and towns, although ACGA staff have told me privately that there has been no comprehensive inventory and that the number may be twice as large. In 1993 the ACGA received approximately eight hundred requests for information on starting up community garden programs, either at the neighborhood or city level. In its 1994 survey, the National Gardening Association found that 6.7 million households, which are not currently engaged in gardening, would be interested in community gardening if there were a garden nearby.

As institutional depth is being built into this movement, another dimension, intellectual rigor, is on the rise. Funders and city officials (and even those of us who are believers) have begun seeking more exact measures of the benefits of community gardens. "Increasingly," writes David Malakoff, the managing editor of *Community Greening Review*, "politicians, developers, and taxpayers are demanding evidence—facts and figures—that greening is a good investment." The supply side of this process of evidence-gathering is also growing: Over the past year, a half-dozen students from the fields of public health, environmental policy, sustainable agriculture, and geography have contacted me in the course of their research on the community health and welfare benefits of community gardens.

I have always encouraged students to use quantitative as well as qualitative data in analyzing the benefits and costs of technologies and public projects; but I also acknowledge the dilemmas inherent in buying into cost/benefit analysis. For one, there is the (often illusory) expectation that impressive numbers will result in favorable outcomes. The very program that systematically documented the market value of the food grown by low-income urban gardeners and found a six dollar return for each dollar invested in 1989—the Urban Gardening Program of the United States Department of Agriculture—essentially lost its federal funding in 1993. For another, tangibles, such as crime statistics, and market goods, such as food produced, are generally easier to quantify and express in economic terms than intangibles such as community-building, leadership, self-esteem, and peace of mind. What happens when the dollar value of a benefit is underestimated, unknown, or impossible to calculate? Do we lose the twenty gardens of the four-acre Cornell Oasis to sixty townhouses because the value of its biodiversity is not possible to calculate in dollars, and the benefit of tranquillity to the gardeners is estimated to be 1/1000th of the return on the development project?

I wholeheartedly agree with the caveat expressed by the researchers at Rutgers University and Cooperative Extension who have surveyed gardeners at the New Brunswick Community Gardens and Nutrition Program, which is that the pursuit of evaluation tools should be a secondary goal to the implementation of vigorous community garden programs. With or without definitive academic proof that the gardens build self-esteem and neighborliness and improve nutrition, we ought to invest in and support them. Community gardens are one of our most participatory local civic institutions, and among the few living landscapes of our cities. Let us study them, with the eye and the heart as well as the calculator, primarily to protect and promote them. And let us listen to the gardeners whose stories may hold more strategic and political power than the rigor of quantitative data.

Rarely have I heard love invoked so thoughtfully as when community gardeners at Thomas Flannery Apartments for Senior Citizens explained why they garden. Not an amorous love, Louis Berkhalter's and Presley Robinson, Jr.'s peace and prayerfulness when gardening is more the expression of a spiritual love. Sometimes the love shown is light and charming, as when Mary Dingle sings and talks to her plants. Wes Wagar didn't use the word love, but he guided me by flashlight one evening through his garden of wild edibles on Maxwell Street, including a small mulberry tree and a few cultivated vegetables, with an air of contemplative respect that one could call love. As Cheryl Johnson and Orrin Williams drove a small group of us through the polluted, doughnut-shaped environs of industrial South Chicago, Orrin spoke compassionately on behalf of stressed vegetation near industrial sites: "You can just see its suffering."

How do we measure the humanizing love that plants and gardens cultivate in people, and the value of that love for making cities livable? Love like this must be witnessed and fostered. Obstacles—whether a lack of secure land, water, seeds, or horticultural knowledge—should be cleared out of its way.

NOTES

INTRODUCTION

p. ix   *"wilderness ethic is silent or unhelpful"*   Pollan, p. 265.

p. xii   *"and I think this is it"*   Kinzer, p. K1.

p. xiv   *"social development can take place"*   Lewis, p. 56.

p. xv   *"twentieth-century land greed"*   Warner, *To Dwell is to Garden*, p. xii.

p. xvii   *"the soil we live on"*   Hyams, *Soil and Civilization*, p. vii.

HARLEM: FLOWERS FEED THE SOUL

All quotations from members of the Greening of Harlem and WHEAct are taken from a series of interviews I conducted in Harlem during August 1992, November 1992, and June 1993. In November 1992 I worked with a film crew hired by the American Institute of Architects (AIA) to develop a segment on the Greening of Harlem for the AIA national teleconference on the urban environment, which was aired spring 1993.

p. 16   *safety surface*   In Barlow's Injury Prevention Program, concrete and macadam playground surfaces are replaced with Child Safe Safety Surface, a poured-in-place, seamless rubberized material that incorporates crumbled recycled tire into its surface layer. Metal play equipment is replaced with rubber, plastic, and wood counterparts.

p. 19   *"commitment to place and community"*   Leavitt and Saegert, p. 4.

p. 23   *"appreciation conferred on them"*   Jacobs, p. 89.

p. 25   *Mount Morris*   Goldberger, p. 293. One guide to the city notes that this rocky outcrop squeezed out of surrounding flat land creates a sight not seen elsewhere in Manhattan—a public square that, with hilly terrain in its center, cannot be seen as a totality.

p. 26   *"transition to a black neighborhood"*   Landmarks Preservation Commission, p. 5.

p. 26 *"a decline in housing units"*   New York City Department of City Planning, pp. 6–8.

p. 27   *"first-rate urban sculpture"*   Goldberger, p. 294.

p. 33   *children who play at the park.* In December 1993 the City of New York settled favorably for the West Harlem community the lawsuit filed by WHEAct with the Natural Resources Defense Council (NRDC) against the city over the North River sewage treatment plant. According to the terms of the agreement, the city must invest some $55 million into repair of the plant to mitigate the odors (although success is questionable). A $1.1 million trust fund is being established for WHEAct and NRDC to administer on community, environmental, and health concerns in West Harlem, including community gardens.

p. 34   *"These are the indignities"*   Miller, p. 20.

p. 34   *worst slum in New York City*   Gilbert Osofsky writes that during the span of a decade (the 1920s), Harlem devolved from a mixed ethnic neighborhood (which had replaced the original white upper-class community) to the most appalling slum in the city. He cites a constellation of forces that conspired against the newly arrived blacks. Between 1920 and 1930 the Harlem population expanded 115 percent, growing from 152,467 to 327,706. Rents in Harlem doubled from 1919 to 1927 while only menial, low-paying jobs were open to blacks. Tenants took in lodgers; spacious Victorian brownstones were subdivided into congested and unsanitary rooming houses; buildings were increasingly allowed to deteriorate by slum landlords (white and black) who enjoyed an appreciating real estate market in Harlem. During this same period, the death rate in Harlem from all causes "was 42 per cent in excess of that of the entire city" (Osofsky, p. 355). Harlem was preyed on by parasites who exploited the community's poverty: A study by Dr. Ernest R. Alexander found extensive houses of prostitution in Harlem neighborhoods, "more than 90 per cent of these . . . institutions were owned and managed by whites" (Ibid., p. 362).

p. 34   *"bare-legged children"*   Caro, p. 512.

p. 35   *"Robert Moses spent millions"*   Miller, pp. 12–13.

p. 35   *"there wasn't a single patch of green"*   Caro, p. 493.

p. 36   *"race and income are significantly correlated"*   Maller, p. 2.

p. 36   *"transformed into parkland"*   Ibid., p. 82.

SAN FRANCISCO: A CLASS OF STARS

All quotations from members of the Horticulture Project, the Garden Project, the Tree Corps, and the San Francisco Sheriff's Department are taken from a series of interviews I conducted between March 21 and March 24, 1994. Any material quoted in the section "The Beginnings" (pp. 57–60), is taken from a talk given by Cathrine Sneed and a film presentation of *Growing Season* on November 18, 1993, at Harvard University.

p. 46   *"As a community"*   Rideau, p. 80. Wilbert Rideau is editor of the *Angolite*, the Louisiana State Penitentiary newsmagazine, and in prison since 1962 for murder. He writes that the most effective deterrent to crime in society is to *"prevent* (his emphasis) the criminal act in the first place." Teach young people, he argued in a *Time* magazine essay, "to respect the humanity of others and to handle disputes without violence . . . Educate and equip them with the skills to pursue their life ambitions in a meaningful way." There are, he added, some who should not be returned to society—"serial killers, serial rapists, professional hit men and the like"; but these are a small proportion of the prison population. The majority of people in prisons are "unskilled, impulsive, and uneducated misfits, mostly black, who had done dumb, impulsive things—failures, rejects from the larger society." (In 1992 the United States imprisoned black men at five times the rate of South Africa.) He argued that prisons have a role in public safety but have only limited value in providing our society with insightful human beings who respect themselves and others. "As a community, we must address the adverse life circumstances that spawn criminality" (Rideau, p. 80).

p. 47   *"world's largest and most crowded"*   Rice, p. 43.

p. 47   *One commentator attributes*   Ibid., pp. 42–43.

p. 47   *"the ideological merging"*   Davis, p. 21.

p. 47   *"sexual abuse during childhood"*   Giobbe, p. 9.

p. 49   *"People come in here"*   Silvern, A-13.

p. 49   *"dark and dusty and urine-smelling cellar"*   Kozol, p. 85.

p. 55   *"sharing it with them"*   Waters, p. 3.

p. 64   *"I heard the president"*   Wellington.

p. 67   *"The land was dying for want of trees"*   Giono, p. 19.

p. 67   *"sprung from the hands and the soul"*   Ibid., p. 25.

p. 68   *horticultural version of New Age spirituality*   Silvern, A-1.

p. 69   *"incessant struggle"*   Freire, p. 33.

PHILADELPHIA: A CITY OF NEIGHBORHOODS

All quotations from members of Philadelphia Green are taken from a series of interviews I conducted in March, July, and September, 1993.

p. 73   *"This is what the city gardener knows"*   Friedlaender, p. 158.

p. 75   *after the Incas and Aztecs*   Hyams, *A History of Gardens and Gardening*. The Aztec city of Tenochtitlán, on the site now occupied by Mexico City, had roof gardens in dense neighborhoods, gardens teeming with flowers, vegetables, and medicinal herbs cultivated around peasant huts, private courtyard gardens, orchards, forests and *chinampas*, or gardens floating upon the lake on which the city was built. The *chinampas* base was woven of reeds and rushes and then piled with soil and organic muck. Vegetables, flowers, and small trees were planted; a hut was built for the resident gardener. With a long pole, the *chinampas* gardener could punt the lacustrine garden nearer to market or to track the diurnal sun. The descriptions of this marvelous mosaic of woodlands, water, cultivated plains, and garden city were recorded by Cortez who, with the Spanish army, plundered this civilization.

p. 76   *In 1990 taxpayers . . . paid more money*   Dreier, pp. 20-25. The Association of Community Organizations for Reform Now (ACORN) surveyed 120 banks, thrifts, and mortgage companies in 23 U.S. cities to examine disparities in lending between whites and minorities in the years 1990, 1991, and 1992. Using Home Mortgage Disclosure Act data, ACORN found that overall these banks reject blacks and Hispanics for mortgages at a much higher rate than white applicants (five banks rejected black and Hispanic applicants seven times as often or more as whites in 1992).

Among cities with high minority populations, Philadelphia ranked best in the survey. "The four Philadelphia lenders studied [Corestates, Mellon, Continental, and Meridien] led the country in minority lending. Overall, 43.0% of loans made by the four lenders went to blacks and Hispanics in 1992—an increase from 41.5% in 1991 and 35.6% in 1990. This compares favorably with New York, where only 13.6% of loans originated by the six lenders studied went to blacks and Hispanics, and to Chicago, where 9.4% of loans went to blacks and Hispanics. A long history of community reinvestment activism and long-standing partnerships between community groups and lenders in Philadelphia may explain the unique performance of lenders there" (*Treading Water*, p.3).

p. 81   *Philadelphia was the first large city . . . to mandate recycling*
Minter. Philadelphia has a program for composting organic wastes, including leaves, grass clippings, and wood chips from Fairmount Park activities and private contractors, as well as animal bedding and police horse manure. The public can deposit compostable materials or use the end products. Philadelphia Green supplies community gardens with compost from the Fairmount Park site.

p. 88   *"Perhaps the most significant benefit"*   Patel, p. 8.

p. 89   *eight hundred acres of "farmland"*   United States Department of Agriculture.

p. 89   *"grounded within a community"*   Nabhan, p. 67.

p. 90   *self-determination and productivity*   Patel et al., pp. 20-21.

pp. 90–91   *Listen to the urban gardeners*   Patel, p. 8.

p. 94   *futures of unemployment and further poverty*   National Research Council.

p. 94   *increase of 43 percent since 1987*   *The Philadelphia Inquirer*, p. A4.

p. 94   *"Life did not seem a terrible affair"*   Brown, pp. 18–19.

p.107   *"helping people to help themselves"*   A forerunner of Philadelphia Green was Philadelphia's Neighborhood Park Program, a project of the 1960s, whose purpose was to build vest-pocket playgrounds, sitting areas, and gardens on vacant lots in low-income neighborhoods. This program was directed by social worker Eve Asner and funded with city and federal monies. In a period of two years, 1965–67, Asner built sixty small parks and play spaces. More significantly, she introduced community involvement and ownership into the project: participation by the neighborhood residents in design and construction; partnership between the neighborhood group and the city in initiating and maintaining the park; and openness to additional neighborhood improvements in housing, yards, and other vacant lots. This approach marked a shift in the politics of open space design (Asner).

p. 114   *"place-attachment"*   Hull and Vigo, p. 149.

pp. 114–15   *"The tradition of privatism"*   Warner, *The Private City*, p. 4.

CHICAGO: HORTUS IN URBE

All quotations from members of Cabrini Greens and the Flannery gardeners are taken from a series of interviews I conducted between July 18 and July 23, 1994.

p. 119   *"The activity of restoring"*   Dunn.

p. 119   *"three times the rate of white infants"*   Cauvin, p. 1.

p. 119   *"they are . . . still children"*   Kotlowitz, p. xi.

p. 128   *Chicago's public school system [was] the worst in the country*   Kotlowitz, p. 64.

pp. 128–29   *the main dispute was between two rival gangs*   O'Connor and Lang.

p. 146   *good-spirited, competitive energy*   Robbins, pp. 140-147.

p. 146   *"generous expanses of shunned areas"*   Jacobs, pp. 42–43.

p. 146   *"junk yards and used-car lots"*   Ibid., p. 231.

p. 146   *Urban Resources Initiative*   Frohardt, p. 1-12.

p. 148   *Urban Resource Partnership for Chicago*   Malakoff, pp. 18-23.

WHY SO MANY WOMEN?

p. 151   *"to cultivate their flower gardens"*   Lawrence, p. 2.

p. 151   *"freely, willingly, and with love"*   Ibid., p. 2.

pp. 151–52   *"they garden for love"*   Ibid., p. 3.

p. 152   *Medieval and Renaissance village women*   Bennett, pp. 39-54.

p. 152   *In mid-sixteenth century Germany*   Hyams, *A History of Gardens and Gardening.*

p. 153   *"to read or write"*   Walker, p. 234.

p. 154   *"her personal conception of Beauty"*   Ibid., p. 241.

p. 154   *"a lover of working in the earth"*   Leighton, p. 1.

p. 154   *"enough hope to go on living"*   Ibid., p. 2.

p. 155 *"basic spiritual security on life"*   Ibid., p. 3.

p. 155 *"the power of growth"*   Ibid., p. 8.

p. 155 *"homely act of earthkeeping"*   Morgan, p. 242.

p. 155 *According to United Nations statistics*   Dankelman, pp. 7–28.

p. 156 *about two hundred million*   International Development Research Center, p. 30.

p. 157 *"while they are helping the environment"*   Leary.

p. 157 *"reach out to others"*   Ibid.

Epilogue

p. 160 *"greening is a good investment"*   Malakoff, "What Good Is Community Greening," p. 6.

BIBLIOGRAPHY

American Community Gardening Association. *ACGA Multilogue* and *Community Greening Review*. Philadelphia, 1993–1994.

American Institute of Architects. National Teleconference on the Urban Environment. Washington, D.C., 1993.

Andersen, Phyllis. "The City and the Garden." In *Keeping Eden*, edited by Walter T. Punch. Boston: Little, Brown, 1992.

"Annual Survey of Home Prices." *The Philadelphia Inquirer*, 30 May 1993, p. A4.

Asner, Eve. "Philadelphia's Neighborhood Park Program." In *Small Urban Spaces*, edited by Whitney North Seymour, Jr. New York: New York University Press, 1969.

Association of Community Organizations for Reform Now. *Treading Water*. Washington, D.C.: ACORN, 1993.

Bennett, Jennifer. *Lilies of the Hearth: The Historical Relationship Between Women and Plants*. Ontario: Camden House, 1991.

Brown, Elaine. *A Taste of Power: A Black Woman's Story*. New York: Pantheon, 1992.

Caro, Robert A. *The Power Broker: Robert Moses and the Fall of New York*. New York: Alfred A. Knopf, 1974.

Cauvin, Henri E. "City's Black Infant Death Rate Edges Up." *Chicago Tribune*, 21 July 1994, sec. 2, p. 128.

Dankelman, Irene, and Joan Davidson. *Women and Environment in the Third World*. London: Earthscan, 1987.

Davidson, Leslie L. et al. "The Impact of the Safe Kids/Healthy Neighborhoods Injury Prevention Program in Harlem, 1988 through 1991." *American Journal of Public Health* 84, no. 4 (April 1994): 580–86.

Davis, Angela. Keynote Address given at Conference on Black Women in the Academy, M.I.T., January 1994. In *Sojourner: The Women's Forum* (July 1994): 21.

Dreier, Peter. "Bush to Cities: Drop Dead." *The Progressive* (July 1992): 20–23.

Dunn, Ken. "A Challenge to Restore Our Habitat." *Chicago Tribune*, 30 March 1994, sec. 1, p. 22.

Freire, Paulo. *Pedagogy of the Oppressed*. New York: Continuum, 1985.

Friedlaender, Bilge. *The Role of Horticulture in Human Well-Being and Social Development*, edited by Diane Relf. Oregon: Timber Press, 1992.

Frohardt, Katherine Elsom. *Case Studies of Entrepreneurial Community Greening Projects*. Philadelphia: American Community Gardening Association, February 1993.

Giobbe, Evelina. "Juvenile Prostitution: A Profile of Recruitment." WHISPER VIII, no. 2 (Winter 1993): 9.

Giono, Jean. *The Man Who Planted Trees*. White River Junction, Vermont: Chelsea Green, 1985.

Goldberger, Paul. *The City Observed*. New York: Random House, 1979.

Hlubik, William T. et al. "Incorporating Research with Community Gardens: The New Brunswick Community Gardening and Nutrition Program." In *The Healing Dimensions of People-Plant Relations*, proceedings of a research symposium edited by Mark Francis, Patricia Lindsey, and Jay Stone Rice. University of California, Davis: Center for Design Research, 1994.

Holloway, Lynette. "A Park, However It Smells, Blossoms on the River." *The New York Times*, 28 May 1993, pp. B1, B3.

Hull, R. Bruce, and Gabriela Vigo. "Urban Nature, Place Attachment, Health and Well-Being." In *The Role of Horticulture in Human Well-Being and Social Development*, edited by Diane Relf. Oregon: Timber Press, 1992.

Hyams, Edward. *A History of Gardens and Gardening*. London: J.M. Dent, 1971.

——. *Soil and Civilization*. New York: Harper, 1976.

International Development Research Centre. "Urban Food Self-Reliance: Significance and Prospects." *IRDC Reports* 21, no. 3 (October): 2–5. Ottawa: International Development Research Centre, 1993.

Jacobs, Jane. *The Death and Life of Great American Cities*. New York: Vintage, 1961.

Kinzer, Stephen. "Dread of Builders in a Garden City." *The New York Times*, 18 February 1994, p. K1.

Kotlowitz, Alex. *There Are No Children Here*. New York: Anchor, 1991.

Kozol, Jonathan. *Death at an Early Age*. New York: Plume, 1985 (1967).

——. *Illiterate America*. New York: Penguin, 1985.

171

Landmarks Preservation Commission. "Mount Morris Park Historic District Designation Report." City of New York, 1971.

Lawrence, Elizabeth. *Gardening for Love: The Market Bulletins*. Edited, with an introduction by Allen Lacy. Durham: Duke University Press, 1987.

Leary, Kevin. "Green Giants at Jailhouse Garden." *San Francisco Chronicle*, 15 May 1991, p. 10.

Leavitt, Jacqueline, and Susan Saegert. *From Abandonment to Hope: Community-Households in Harlem*. New York: Columbia University Press, 1990.

Leighton, Clare. "The Philosophy of Gardening." Berkshire, England: Croft Publications, 1991.

Lewis, Charles. "Effects of Plants and Gardening in Creating Interpersonal and Community Well-Being." In *The Role of Horticulture in Human Well-Being and Social Development*, edited by Diane Relf. Oregon: Timber Press, 1992.

Malakoff, David. "Chicago, Illinois: City in a Garden." *Community Greening Review* 4 (1994): 18–23.

———. "What Good Is Community Greening?" *Community Greening Review* 5 (1995): 4–11.

Maller, Lisa. "New York City's Parkland: A Case Study for Redressing Environmental Inequities." Master's Thesis, M.I.T., 1993.

Miller, Vernice. "Planning, Power, and Politics: A Case Study of the Land Use and Siting History of the North River Water Pollution Control Plant." Unpublished paper, 1993.

Minter, Susan. "Recycling and Economic Development: A Case Study of Philadelphia and Policy Implications for Medium-size Cities." Unpublished Master's Thesis, M.I.T., 1991.

Morgan, Robin. "Upstairs in the Garden." In *Upstairs in the Garden: Poems Selected and New 1968–1988*. New York: W.W. Norton, 1990.

Murphy, Rose. "Keeping a Good Thing Going: A History of Community Gardening in the United States." *Green-Up Times* 3, no. 2 (Summer 1991): 1–2.

Nabhan, Gary Paul. *Enduring Seeds: Native American Agriculture and Wild Plant Conservation*. San Francisco: North Point Press, 1989.

National Research Council. *Losing Generations: Adolescents in High-Risk Settings*. Washington, D.C., 1993.

New York City Department of City Planning. "Neighborhood Land Disposition Plan: South Central Harlem." City of New York, Fall 1992.

O'Connor, Phillip J., and Clarence Lang. "Gangs Drive off Muslim Guards." *Chicago Sun-Times*, 22 July 1994 (metro edition), p. 5.

Osofsky, Gilbert. "Harlem: The Making of a Ghetto — Negro New York, 1890–1930." In *The City in American Life*, edited by Paul Kramer and Frederick L. Holborn. New York: Putnam, 1970.

Patel, Ishwarbhai C. "Gardening's Socioeconomic Impacts." *Journal of Extension* (Winter 1991): 7–8.

Patel, Ishwarbhai C. et al. *Urban Gardening Program Evaluation, Rutgers Cooperative Extension of Essex County*. Department of Agricultural-Resource Management Agents, Cook College, June 1989.

Perlman, Janice E. "A Dual Strategy for Deliberate Social Change in Cities." *Cities* (February 1990): 3–15.

Platt, Rutherford H. et al. *The Ecological City*. Amherst: University of Massachusetts Press, 1994.

Pollan, Michael. "Afterword: The Garden's Prospects in America." In *Keeping Eden*, edited by Walter Punch. Boston: Little, Brown, 1992.

Raver, Anne. "When Hope Falters, Balm for the Soul." *The New York Times*, 29 December 1994, pp. C1, C6.

Rice, Jay Stone. *Self Development and Horticultural Therapy in a Jail Setting*. Unpublished Ph.D. dissertation, The Professional School of Psychology, 1993.

Rideau, Wilbert. "Why Prisons Don't Work." *Time*, 21 March 1994, p. 80.

Robbins, Ira S. "Tenants' Gardens in Public Housing." In *Small Urban Spaces*, edited by Whitney North Seymour, Jr. New York: New York University Press, 1969.

Rosen, Martin J., quoted in William Poole and Susan Ives, "Building Hope in America's Cities," *Land and People* 5, no. 1 (Fall 1993): 2–5.

Seitz, John M. *Beyond Pastoralism: Through Community Gardens to a Model of Sustainable Design and a Metaphor of Integration*. Master's Thesis, M.I.T., 1993.

Seymour, Whitney North, Jr., ed. *Small Urban Spaces*. New York: New York University Press, 1969.

Shiffman, Ronald. "The Vest-Pocket Park as an Instrument of Social Change." In *Small Urban Spaces*, edited by Whitney North Seymour, Jr. New York: New York University Press, 1969.

Silvern, Drew. "Self-Respect Blooms in Inmates' Garden." *The San Diego Union–Tribune*, 4 January 1994, pp. A-1, A-13.

United States Department of Agriculture Extension Service. "Urban Gardening Program FY 1989 Report." Washington, D.C., 1989.

Walker, Alice. *In Search of Our Mothers' Gardens*. New York: Harcourt Brace Jovanovich, 1983.

Waring, Marilyn. *If Women Counted*. San Francisco: Harper and Row, 1988.

Warner, Sam Bass, Jr. *To Dwell Is to Garden*. Boston: Northeastern University Press, 1987.

———. *The Private City: Philadelphia in Three Periods of Its Growth*. Revised Edition. Philadelphia: University of Pennsylvania Press, 1987.

Waters, Alice. "Making Food the Educational Priority." AIWF Conference, *Children's Education: Feeding Our Future*, 1994.

Wellington, Nicholas. *Growing Season*. Oley, Pennsylvania: Bullfrog Films, 1992. Film.

RESOURCES

This is not an exhaustive list of organizations or materials. To find a community gardening organization in your city, contact the American Community Gardening Association.

Organizations

American Community Gardening Association (ACGA)
325 Walnut Street
Philadelphia, PA 19106-2777
FAX 215-625-9392
The most comprehensive community gardening organization in the United States. Members receive monthly publications as well as access to the network of other members with expertise on community gardens and to ACGA educational materials.

Cabrini Greens
c/o Jack Davis
Edwin C. Sigel, Ltd.
3400 Dundee Road, Suite 180
Northbrook, IL 60062

The Garden Project
35 South Park
San Francisco, CA 94107

The Greening of Harlem Coalition
c/o Bernadette Cozart
Harlem Hospital KP 17103
506 Lenox Avenue
New York, New York 10037

Penn State Urban Gardening Program
4601 Market Street Third Floor
Philadelphia, PA 19139
(215) 560-4167

Philadelphia Green
Pennsylvania Horticulture Society
325 Walnut Street
Philadelphia, PA 19106-2777
(215) 625-8280
Neighborhood Gardens Association/A Philadelphia Land Trust
(215) 625-8264

Guides and Information

Starting a Community Garden

Fact sheet available from American Community Gardening Association. Includes guidance on organizational structure, site selection and development, insurance, day-to-day management, and horticultural resources.

"Creating Community Gardens," a handbook for planning and creating community gardens. Covers the same topics in the ACGA fact sheet but offers more detail particularly about horticulture and garden care. Available for three dollars from:

Minnesota State Horticultural Society
Minnesota Green
1970 Folwell Avenue #161
St. Paul, Minnesota 55108

School Gardens

GrowLab, the National Gardening Association's plant-based education program. Includes innovative instructional resources for the classroom, youth garden grants program, in-service workshop materials, newsletter, and a national network of educators, community partners, and funders exchanging ideas about education though horticulture. Write or call:

National Gardening Association
180 Flynn Avenue
Burlington, VT 05401
1-800-538-7476

Reference Manual

Philadelphia Green Gardeners' Guide, a collection of more than 150 fact sheets from Philadelphia's community gardening organizations and greening programs nationwide. Topics include horticulture and garden maintenance, youth and craft activities, and organizational guidance. An indexed monthly gardening calendar gives suggestions for year-round activities. Additional handouts provided to subscribers as they are developed. For information and price, write:

PHS/Philadelphia Green
Education Department
325 Walnut Street
Philadelphia, PA 19106-2777

Film

Growing Season

Produced by Nicholas Wellington. 1992. 25 minute video on the Horticulture Project at the San Francisco County Jail in San Bruno in which Cathrine Sneed and many of her students speak about the garden as transforming their lives. Available from:

Bullfrog Films
P.O. Box 149
Oley, PA 19547
1-800-543-3764
Purchase price: $195
Rental price: $40
Add $5.00 for shipping

INDEX

Italics indicate references to photographs.

Q

R

S

T

185

Chelsea Green Publishing Company

THE SUSTAINABLE WORLD IS ONE IN WHICH ALL HUMAN ACTIVITIES ARE designed to co-exist and cooperate with natural processes, rather than dominate nature. Resources are recognized to be finite. Consumption and production are carefully and consciously balanced so that all of the planet's species can thrive in perpetuity.

Chelsea Green specializes in providing the information people need to create and prosper in such a world.

Sustainable Living has many facets. Chelsea Green's celebration of the sustainable arts has led us to publish trend-setting books about organic gardening, solar electricity and renewable energy, innovative building techniques, regenerative forestry, local and bioregional democracy, and whole foods. The company's published works, while intensely practical, are also entertaining and inspirational, demonstrating that an ecological approach to life is consistent with producing beautiful, lucid, and useful books, videos, and audio tapes.

For more information about Chelsea Green, or to request a free catalog, call (800) 639–4099, or write to us at P.O. Box 428, White River Junction, VT 05001.

Chelsea Green's bestselling titles include:

The Man Who Planted Trees	Jean Giono
The New Organic Grower	Eliot Coleman
Beyond the Limits	Meadows, Meadows, and Randers
Loving and Leaving the Good Life	Helen Nearing
Wind Power for Home and Business	Paul Gipe
The Independent Home	Michael Potts
The Contrary Farmer	Gene Logsdon
Solar Gardening	Leandre and Gretchen Poisson
The Straw Bale House	Swentzell Steen, Steen, and Bainbridge.
The Rammed Earth House	David Easton